2010

＃1500

ALTADENA LIBRARY DISTRICT

3 2270 00300 8509

D0012769

0 5 2009

World's End

Fin de mundo

Spanish
861
NER

2169367788

PABLO NERUDA
World's End

TRANSLATED BY WILLIAM O'DALY

COPPER CANYON PRESS

PORT TOWNSEND, WASHINGTON

Copyright 1968 by Pablo Neruda and Fundación Pablo Neruda
Translation copyright 2009 by William O'Daly

Printed in the United States of America

Cover art: Galen Garwood, "Crash," 2005.
Photograph, 12 x 10 inches.

This translation is based on the 2004 edition of *Fin de mundo*, from Debolsillo, Buenos Aires, Argentina. That edition, with a foreword by Carlos Monsiváis, edited and with notes by Hernán Loyola, follows the text of two earlier editions and ultimately the fourth Losada edition (1973) of Neruda's *Obras completas*, all containing revisions and corrections made by Neruda to the text of the first edition of *Fin de mundo*, originally published by Losada in 1969.

Excerpts of the translated poem were first published in *Oregon Literary Review* and *Virginia Quarterly Review*.

Copper Canyon Press is in residence at Fort Worden State Park in Port Townsend, Washington, under the auspices of Centrum. Centrum is a gathering place for artists and creative thinkers from around the world, students of all ages and backgrounds, and audiences seeking extraordinary cultural enrichment.

LIBRARY OF CONGRESS CATALOGING-IN-PUBLICATION DATA
Neruda, Pablo, 1904–1973.
[Fin de mundo. English and Spanish]
World's end / Pablo Neruda; translated by William O'Daly.
p. cm.
ISBN 978-1-55659-282-9 (pbk. : alk. paper)
I. O'Daly, William. II. Title.

PQ8097.N4F513 2009
861'.62—dc22

2008034637

9 8 7 6 5 4 3 2 FIRST PRINTING

COPPER CANYON PRESS
Post Office Box 271
Port Townsend, Washington 98368
www.coppercanyonpress.org

I dedicate this translation of *Fin de mundo*
to my family and friends

CONTENTS

III

IV

V

VI

VII

Translator's Acknowledgments

World's End (*Fin de mundo*) is my eighth and final translation of
Pablo Neruda's late and posthumous work, which series has roots as
far back as 1976, and in certain ways earlier than that. I have been
afforded ample opportunity to offer my vision of Neruda's last years
and, as best as I could, sing along in English, and I have been forever
changed, and honored by the large community of hands that has
helped to shape the translations, the books, and the project. Reed
Ellis Aubin generously lent keen editorial expertise and an ear to both
the Spanish and the English in making this translation as precise as
possible, offering indispensable assistance in bringing the original
poem to life in English. Professor Jaime Concha, of the University of
California at San Diego, kindly offered his thoughts on certain pas-
sages that resist translation, providing clarifications and sometimes
words meant to serve as a life jacket against the original's depths.
I thank my friend and longtime editor David Caligiuri, for the intel-
ligence, heart, and grace he brings to his work and to mine. Sam
Hamill and Tree Swenson, whose vision and hard work developed
and sustained Copper Canyon Press for so many years, committed to

publishing this series some twenty-five years ago, and to them I am forever grateful. The staff at Copper Canyon Press, and its executive editor, Michael Wiegers, continues to provide a home for the series, which has greatly benefited from their expertise, commitment, and gracious spirit. For their generous support, which made possible this translation of *Fin de mundo,* I am grateful to the National Endowment for the Arts.

To my wife, Kristine Iwersen O'Daly, and to our daughter, Kyra Gray O'Daly: I have no words by which I can begin to give back what you have given me in support of this work that has shaped our daily life. I deeply appreciate your understanding and your patience over the previous two years while I finished the series, and I am blessed by your intelligence, sensitive editorial assistance, and love. To my parents, William L. and Madeline M. O'Daly, and to my siblings, Daniel and Deborah, and their families, and to our extended family, your support over the years has meant the world.

INTRODUCTION

I have faith in Chile and its destiny. Other men will
overcome this dark and bitter moment when treason
seeks to prevail. Keep in mind that, much sooner than later,
great avenues will again be opened, through which will pass
the free man, to construct a better society.

SALVADOR ALLENDE, president of Chile,
September 11, 1973

Pablo Neruda wrote *Fin de mundo* (*World's End*) in 1968 and 1969, weaving together public and personal experience on his precisely tuned zither, and published it in the latter year. Musically refined and thematically orchestrated, this book-length poem is an often startling historical journey through social and political disillusionment. Much like *Canto general*, his epic of the South American continent, this late work was impelled by the process of clarifying experience in the cold fires of the imagination; by the pursuit of common cause and brotherhood; and by his intuitive sense of the composition and the qualities, the weight and the sound of the bellflower and the planets, of sorrow and stone. Neruda's kinship with beautiful or intriguing objects, with the material world and the color blue, his connectedness with friends and enemies, firmly ground this sustained articulation of his utterly self-aware, humane, and at times surrealistic journey through the absurdly violent twentieth century.

The century is defined by wrenching polarities: "cosmic men" walked on the moon, and millions of children died of shrapnel, radiation, starvation, or gas. In *World's End,* an intricate wedding of opposites arrives at a single necessity, celebrating our distinctiveness yet holding us accountable to a singular morality, which is the sentient toll of the nouns we choose to become and the verbs we choose to live.

> All leaves are this leaf,
> all petals are this flower,
> and abundance a lie.
> For all fruit is the same,
> the trees are one, alone,
> and the earth, a single flower.
>
> ("The Rose of the
> Herbalist: Unity")

Neruda constellates his shortcomings, his mistakes, and his relationship to forgetting in the poem's intellectual-emotional landscape, doing so even as he honors his beliefs. Shaped by the poverty and the tenacious spirit of people who lived by their hands, of those who built roads, sewed shirts, assembled brooms—in Burma, in Ceylon, in Singapore where he served as consul—of the day laborers, miners, porters, pickers, and millworkers of his beloved Chile, his core beliefs never changed. Even later, as he came to realize his own mistaken loyalties and brokered an uneasy truce with his contradictions, the lasting tragedy of the Spanish Civil War continued to nest in his heart— the execution of his good friend Federico García Lorca by Falangists, the death of Miguel Hernández in one of Franco's brutal prisons.

And so many died in Vietnamese jungles, in Siberian wastelands, in
Hiroshima and London, in Prague and Berlin.

> But later I came to know
> in the Spain of my sorrows
> the smoke of annihilation,
> and even now I hate that memory
> because no smoke is more bitter
> than the needless smoke of war.
>
> ("Bomb I")

In *World's End,* Neruda seeks to revive hope that a better socie-
ty will grow from the sacrifices of the brave ones, from the "shackled
poets of Athens," and from the innumerable innocent, in particular
the children, who die at the hands and by the decisions of colonels or
political serpents who conceive of themselves as righteous or cast
themselves as deities, by those who wreak destruction from a place of
self-delusion or paranoia. Here Neruda "constructs" a sturdy tree
much as did his father—the strict and austere ballast train engineer,
who believed he simply was building a house, "his idea of comfort"—
and somewhat as one of his literary grandfathers, Walt Whitman, did
in *Leaves of Grass.* Indeed, *World's End* makes a place for everyone.

> There is a chain that moors
> with invisible links
> the shadows of all bodies:
> so he who sells his shadow
> sells yours as well as his own.
>
> ("The Passion")

In previous introductions to my Neruda translations, I
sought to tailor discussion to the North American reader and placed
the late and posthumous poetry within the stream of his vast oeuvre.

Carlos Monsiváis's foreword to the 2004 Debolsillo edition of *Fin de mundo,* on which I have based this translation, does a particularly fine job of illustrating how the poem arose from previous works such as the 1960 *Canción de gesta* (*Song of Protest*) and part IV of the third book of *Residencia en la tierra* (*Residence on Earth*), written between 1936 and 1937, but most inevitably from *Canto General,* Neruda's only other book-length poem, which he composed over a much longer duration (1938–1949). Given the historical scope of *Fin de mundo,* the reader might benefit from having this extraordinary work situated within its circumstances and time.

––––

Chile has long been considered the most stable democracy in South America. Yet, a number of times in its history the long and rugged Andean country trod a volcanic rim of social and economic change. With the presidential election of 1970 stirring the air, the Chilean people were divided among three candidates and a wide array of political parties and agendas, new alliances, and long-standing aspirations. Among the Chilean aristocracy and the new upper class, the slightest rumbling was perceived as an ominous threat; among the lower classes and some of the middle class, an opportunity for a more egalitarian society sparked a renewal of hope. In September 1969, Neruda was putting the finishing touches on *Fin de mundo* when he was designated the Communist Party's candidate for the presidency. He had not pursued this, yet he campaigned up and down the country, fulfilling his duty to his party and to the people it represented. He then participated in the dialogue that gave rise to Unidad Popular (a coalition of nineteen parties and organizations representing the working classes), before eventually bowing out and lending his support to the Socialist Party candidate, Salvador Allende Gossens, a physician and longtime senator, advocate of peaceful social and economic change, of democratic institutions and processes.

––––

Such a political climate in Chile had also obtained in 1945, the year that preceded the presidency of Gonzáles Videla, the candidate who had spread hope among the lower classes by casting himself in a populist light. In fact, Videla had been a member of the Radical Party and, subsequent to his election to the Senate and then to the presidency one year later, he appointed three Communist Party members to his cabinet. Not long after taking office, however, he began to turn against those who had elected him in order to unabashedly serve the narrow interests of the Chilean aristocracy and of the "stern capitalists," by Neruda's accounting, in the north. President Videla's betrayal set off strikes and protests, and in late 1947, after he had increased government repression, mine workers commenced another strike in the southern coastal town of Lota. People were arrested and herded onto warships destined for military prisons on the islands of Santa María and Quiriquina. Among those responsible for rounding up prisoners was thirty-three-year-old Augusto Pinochet Ugarte, whom years later President Allende would make the fatal mistake of elevating to commander in chief of the Chilean army. The majority of arrested workers were eventually transported to the Pisagua concentration camp in the Atacama Desert, where they were joined by hundreds of others arrested throughout the country. Pinochet was appointed as head of the Pisagua camp, and then as a chief military delegate of the politically volatile area known as the Emergency Zone, thus beginning his ascent through the chain of command.

In the first days of 1948, Neruda, then a senator representing the mining provinces of Tarapacá and Antofagasta, delivered a speech on the Senate floor that became known as "Yo acuso," a castigation of President Videla for his betrayal and tyrannical rule. The Supreme Court removed Neruda from the Senate and issued an arrest warrant, sending the renowned *poeta del pueblo,* then researching and writing *Canto general,* into hiding in closets and sheds; he relied on friends, and friends of friends, in his loops through Santiago and back out to the countryside. Videla outlawed the Communist Party, a dubious act in any true democracy. And one year after going into hiding, as the police finally closed in, Neruda was driven south into the Lake District and then rode horseback in the company of two vaqueros over the Andes and into exile.

Salvador Allende was no Gonzáles Videla, having for many years spoken and worked on behalf of the under-represented in Chile. His voting record and actions as a senator evinced his declared values and beliefs, his integrity and constancy as a human being and an intellectual, and his fundamental honesty as public servant and politician. After members of the moderate Christian Democratic Party offered support to Allende, if he would pay heed to their agenda after he was elected, Allende received 36 percent of the popular vote, narrowly winning the presidency. This rare and momentous occasion did not arrive for Neruda without his feeling some trepidation regarding what might lie ahead, based on concerns about political elements who vehemently opposed any socialist agenda and about the fragility of the coalition. But one belief spanned much of the continuum of Chilean political thought and allegiance: the country was immune from a phenomenon shared by most other South American countries, the threat of military coup. Most Chileans did not spend much time worrying that their elected government would be unduly influenced by a foreign regime or, even less likely, overthrown from within.

Meanwhile, the Vietnam War raged on, killing hundreds and in some weeks thousands of people despite pleas for peace from North American churches, self-immolation of Buddhist monks while television cameras filmed, massive protests, some violent, and thousands of nonviolent protests by millions of all ages, races, nationalities, and walks of life.

Why go so far to kill?
Why go so far to die?

("Why, Sir?")

A couple of years earlier, the revolutionary fighter Che Guevara, formerly minister of industry in Fidel Castro's Cuba, had been captured by the Bolivian army (assisted by the CIA) and taken to the village of La Higuera, where he was executed. For Neruda, hope outside Chile came in the form of Castro's familiar fatigues. Neruda and many others viewed Castro as reclaiming for impoverished people their small island nation of Cuba, which "stern capitalists" had colonized and which political turpitude, wealthy tourists, and speculators had essentially turned into a brothel. The palaces of human inattention were serenaded by the cries of the poor, by those whose children faced the same daily deprivations. But also, Castro appeared to be an antidote to both "the idolized revolution" and the "patriarchal lie" —the former wielded by bipolar revolutionary leaders turned brutal dictators, the latter a tool of established national leaders exerting their power and furthering their aims. In contrast, Neruda in *World's End* anoints Fidel Castro a genuine man of the people, who was creating on that politically and economically vulnerable island a more equitable and just society.

Throughout the sixties, Neruda reassessed his loyalties and specific actions he had taken in pursuit of practical change, precipitating an inner struggle that pitted the ideological party man against the poet. The central seed of that long, disturbing, and painful struggle turned out to be one of the most brutal dictators of the century, Joseph Stalin, a poor Georgian naively perceived by many as a strong leader who would bring lasting political and economic justice to a nation that had been slowly devoured by the monarchy. Stalin appeared the true revolutionary, an oft-exiled and -imprisoned political fighter whose nature later gave pause to, among others, his former supporter Vladimir Lenin, who wrote that he feared Stalin would use his authority without sufficient discretion. Stalin's betrayals of allies and his prolific crimes against humanity, his "geology of terror," which Neruda describes in "The Worship (II)," were eventually revealed to the world. That revelation was accepted only slowly and skeptically by Neruda and others who wanted to believe in what they thought Stalin stood for and who were wary of Western disinformation campaigns:

> I was unaware of that which we were unaware.
> And that madness, so long lasting,
> was blind and buried
> in its demented grandeur,
> wrapped at times in the war
> or spread in rancor
> by our old enemies.

In contrast, Neruda objected swiftly to Mao Tse-tung, another revolutionary turned tyrant and murderer, who put on "the tunic of the imperials" and set himself up on "the altar."

> Instead of flowers that never
> had a chance to be born,
> his monumental statues
> were planted in the gardens.
> His speeches assembled
> in a little red book
> formed the infallible bottle
> of medicinal pills.
> The fact is, nobody gave orders,
> only that masked man.
> Again, he thought for everyone.

> ("The Worship III")

For Neruda, the question of how to respond to his own mistakes of perception and belief became the question of how to keep hope so as not to lose the will to act. Part of the answer to this quandary resides in the almost peristaltic movement of *World's End,* where each of the poem's twelve sections seeks resolution musically and thematically by opening on the next lightning strike or the next wave, bringing with it fragmentation and connectedness, human beings lost or finding their way; and sometimes another, who struggled on behalf of the many at the cost of imprisonment or death. Elsewhere, Neruda celebrates coleopterans, or love, or he says goodbye to the last of his "sad integrity."

> I returned seeking that scent,
> the red rose of pain
> or the yellow of forgetting
> or the white of sadness
> or the uncommon blue rose:
> certainly, we return only in vain
> to the country of springtime:
> I was so late that the stars
> fell onto the road,
> and I stopped to harvest
> the splendor of the nocturnal wheat.
>
> ("The Rose of the
> Herbalist: The Rose")

So it is of much interest that, in this work of uncompromising honesty recalling "the sad bread of victory" kneaded with blood, Neruda transforms what could be an echo of his 1936 admonishment to the world (Witness the blood of children in Spanish streets!) into the basis for his happiness within his unhappiness, for love.

Come see on the bee
a zither of platinum,
on the zither the honey,
and on the honey the waist
of my transparent love.

("Inside")

If Neruda never allowed disillusionment and heartache to destroy his hope, he credits his powers of renewal, as a man and as a poet, to forgetting. The question of forgetting is one of many dialogues that course through *World's End,* and many readers may find the treatment of the question ironic at best and, at worst, contrary to a poet's charge, perhaps indicative of authoritarian proclivities. Yet, in this passage claiming that "it is better to forget," Neruda describes the discomfort of coming to terms with the enormity of someone he had believed in and had tacitly supported.

I was like iron against this pain,
and registering the torments
inside my skinned soul
after the burden of death,
there came the burden of doubt,
and later it is better to forget
so as to sustain hope.

("The Worship II")

Certainly Neruda did not spend more than a year composing *World's End* so that he might then forget. It is more likely that he sought to avoid emotional and spiritual paralysis, so as to carry on. He may have had no choice but to lift the burden, to arrive at a new configuration of self—based on his enduring core values and beliefs—

by preserving the inexorable truth in poetry. By his doing so, the possibility is sown that people will not forget or ignore the lessons offered by their mistakes, even as tragic events that would rob humanity of hope cyclically come to pass.

> The sun is born of its seed
> to its obligatory brilliance,
> it washes the universe with light,
> lies down each day to die
> under the dark sheets
> of the budding night,
> and to be born again
> it leaves its egg in the dew.
>
> ("Always Being Born")

Four years after Neruda published *Fin de mundo*, top officers from all branches of the Chilean military and the Carabineros waited outside the Palacio de La Moneda in the capital and issued to President Allende a warning that they were ready to attack the building. Backed by the United States and Britain, top Chilean military officers favoring a coup, most notably Pinochet, had murdered or otherwise neutralized those loyal to the standing government or to democratic processes. They offered President Allende safe passage out of the country, but rather than capitulate, Allende made shortly before his death a deeply impassioned plea to the Chilean people to retain faith in their motherland and in themselves, to affirm each day the power of the desire to live as a free people. He told them that those capable of overcoming "this dark and bitter moment" would prevail, and he asked them to hold on to hope.

On June 30, 1969, a few days shy of his sixty-fifth birthday, Neruda told four journalists that *Fin de mundo* would be the gift he would give his readers on that occasion, and yet he also referred to it as a "bitter book." Perhaps when the bitterness visited him, it was integrated into the gift and was transformed:

> Because being born is one thing,
> and a whole other thing is the
>   end of the world
> with its fiery volcanoes
> that proposed giving birth to you.

> ("Book")

Neruda would not live long enough to accept the challenge of keeping his hope alive under the military dictatorship of Augusto Pinochet, he died twelve days after the coup, on September 23, 1973. Yet, incredibly, he wrote fourteen books between the time he finished *Fin de mundo* and his death, clearly retaining both his passion for his work and for life.

> My protagonist has
> no interest in the sky:
> he goes to leave his merchandise
> at the market of Talcachifa,
> and while he multiplies his miseries
> in a rickety car,
> the night enters his eyes,
> his pockets, his hands,
> and he soon feels black:
> he has slowly been consumed
> by the solitude of the land.

> ("The Traveler")

The preceding passage circles back to the first in my series of eight late and posthumous Neruda books, to that often understated book that Robert Pring-Mill characterizes as a poem composed of "little symphonies," *Aún* (*Still Another Day*), which Neruda wrote while taking a break from *Fin de mundo* over a two-day period in July 1969. We come to see in these books that "the solitude of the land," as he calls it in "The Traveler," is essentially the solitude of self, an isolation that binds us to one another, breathing both our solitude and a shared destiny. Neruda took this separateness when he left Temuco for Santiago at age nineteen: it split like a seed within him when he visited the houses of the impoverished miners who elected him senator. Later, he carried that investiture in his saddlebags, in the form of a typewriter, as he rode into exile.

Singing his song, Neruda composes the poem that is *World's End* from remembrance, recalling the most difficult and painful events in a century of deflection and denial, a century rife with bloodshed and lies. But it is also a century that, for all its horror, inspires through the aegis of those whose personal lives intersected with historical events and who faced down their isolation and fear to make room for difficult truths, who in their solitude bore responsibility and admitted how so much depends on concentric communities, the smaller within the larger, each also a reflection of the other.

WILLIAM O'DALY
SPRING 2008

World's End

Fin de mundo

PRÓLOGO

Qué siglo permanente!

Preguntamos:
Cuándo caerá? Cuándo se irá de bruces
al compacto, al vacío?
A la revolución idolatrada?
O a la definitiva
mentira patriarcal?
Pero lo cierto
es que no lo vivimos
de tanto que queríamos vivirlo.

Siempre fue una agonía:
siempre estaba muriéndose:
amanecía con luz y en la noche era sangre:
llovía en la mañana, por la tarde lloraba.

Los novios encontraron
que la torta nupcial tenía heridas
como una operación de apendicitis.

Subían hombres cósmicos
por una escala de fuego
y cuando ya tocábamos
los pies de la verdad
ésta se había marchado a otro planeta.

Y nos mirábamos unos a otros con odio:
los capitalistas más severos no sabían qué hacer:

PROLOGUE

THE DOOR

What a ceaseless century!

We ask:
When will it fall? When will it wind up facedown
in compactedness, in emptiness?
In the idolized revolution?
Or in the ultimate
patriarchal lie?
But what's certain
is that we did not live it
because we wanted so much to live it.

It was always agony,
it was always dying,
it dawned with light and in the night was blood:
it rained in the morning, by afternoon it cried.

Newlyweds discovered
that the wedding cake had wounds
as from an appendectomy.

Cosmic men climbed
a ladder of fire
and when at last we were touching
the feet of truth
it had marched off, to another planet.

And we looked at one another with hatred:
stern capitalists didn't know what to do:

se habían fatigado del dinero
porque el dinero estaba fatigado
y partían los aviones vacíos.
Aún no llegaban los nuevos pasajeros.

Todos estábamos esperando
como en las estaciones en las noches de invierno:
esperábamos la paz
y llegaba la guerra.

Nadie quería decir nada: todos
tenían miedo de comprometerse:
de un hombre a otro se agravó la distancia
y se hicieron tan diferentes los idiomas
que terminaron por callarse todos
o por hablarse todos a la vez.

Sólo los perros siguieron ladrando
en la noche silvestre de las naciones pobres.
Y una mitad del siglo fue silencio:
la otra mitad los perros que ladraban
en la noche silvestre.

No se caía el diente amargo.

Siguió crucificándonos.

Nos abría una puerta, nos seguía
con una cola de cometa de oro
nos cerraba una puerta, nos pegaba
en el vientre con una culata,
nos libertaba un preso y cuando
lo levantábamos sobre los hombros

they had grown weary of money
because the money was weary
and the airplanes departed empty.
No new passengers showed up.

We all were waiting
as in stations on long winter nights:
we were waiting for peace
and war was arriving.

No one wanted to utter a word: all
were afraid of endangering themselves:
between one man and the next distance grew
and languages became so very different
that everyone wound up silent
or all conversing at once.

Only the dogs carried on, barking
in the wild night of impoverished nations.
One half of this century was silence:
the other half, dogs barking
in the wild night.

The bitter tooth did not fall.

It went on tormenting us.

It would open a door for us, follow us
with a tail of a golden comet,
close a door on us, jab
us in the belly with a rifle butt,
release for us a prisoner, and while
we were hoisting him to our shoulders

se tragaba a un millón el calabozo,
otro millón salía desterrado,
luego un millón entraba por un horno
y se convertía en ceniza.

Yo estoy en la puerta partiendo
y recibiendo a los que llegan.

Cuando cayó la Bomba
(hombre, insectos, peces calcinados)
pensamos irnos con el atadito,
cambiar de astro y de raza.
Quisimos ser caballos, inocentes caballos.
Queríamos irnos de aquí.
Lejos de aquí, más lejos.

No sólo por el exterminio,
no sólo se trataba de morir
(fue el miedo nuestro pan de cada día)
sino que con dos pies ya no podíamos
caminar. Era grave
esta vergüenza
de ser hombres
iguales
al desintegrador y al calcinado.

Y otra vez, otra vez.
Hasta cuándo otra vez?

Ya parecía limpia la aurora
con tanto olvido con que la limpiamos
cuando matando aquí matando allá,
continuaron absortos

the prisons were swallowing another million,
another million were refugees fleeing,
then a million were entering an oven
and turning to ash.

In the doorway, I am leaving
and welcoming those who arrive.

When the Bomb dropped
(people, insects, incinerated fish)
we thought to leave with a hobo's bundle,
for a change of heavenly body and race.
We wished to be horses, guileless horses.
We wanted to go away from here.
Far from here, and farther still.

Not only because of extermination,
it was not just about dying
(fear was our daily bread),
but that with two feet we were no longer able
to walk. It was a solemn
shame,
being men
exactly like
the disintegrator and the carbonized.

And again, again,
again, until *when?*

The dawn seemed clean already,
so much forgetting did we clean it with
while killing here and killing there—
entranced, countries

los países
fabricando amenazas y guardándolas
en el almacén de la muerte.

Sí, se ha resuelto, gracias:
nos queda la esperanza.

Por eso, en la puerta, espero
a los que llegan a este fin de fiesta:
a este fin de mundo.

Entro con ellos pase lo que pase.

Me voy con los que parten
y regreso.

Mi deber es vivir, morir, vivir.

carried on
manufacturing threats and storing them
in the warehouse of death.

Yes, it's been resolved, thank you:
we still have hope.

For that reason, I wait at the gateway
for those who arrive at this festival's end:
at this world's end.

I enter with them, come what may.

I leave with those who set out,
and I return.

My duty is to live, to die, to live.

I

LA PASIÓN

Entrelazado he sido hoy
por un concurso de tinieblas
y a mi edad debo declarar
otros caminos incesantes:
la transformación de las olas,
la veracidad del silencio.

Soy sólo un número caído
de un árbol que no tuvo objeto
porque llegó con sus raíces
al otro lado de la tierra.

Mi cantidad es mi tormento.

No tengo nombre todavía.

Recuerdo que en una ciudad
me dormí esperando el otoño:
me encontraron bajo la nieve
tan congelado de blancura
que allí sigo siendo una estatua
sin dirección ni movimiento.

Mi vocación más verdadera
fue llegar a ser un molino:
estudié cantando en el agua
la razón de la transparencia
y aprendí del trigo abundante
la identidad que se repite.

I

The Passion

Today, I have been entangled
in a congress of shadows,
and to my epoch I must declare
other unceasing roads:
the transformation of the waves,
the truthfulness of silence.

I am only a number fallen
from a tree that had no purpose
because it reached with its roots
to the other side of the earth.

My magnitude is my torment.

I still don't have a name.

I remember that in a city
I fell asleep waiting for autumn:
they found me beneath the snow
so frozen white
I remain there still, like a statue
motionless, with no direction.

My truest vocation
was to become a mill:
singing in the water, I studied
the motives of transparency
and learned from the abundant wheat
the identity that repeats itself.

———

Así llegué a ser lo que soy:

el corazón más repartido.

Se sabe que no sólo es tuyo
tu corazón y su alimento:
presumimos que la bondad
no hay que guardarla en los bolsillos:
tus dolores causan dolores.

Tu techo pertenece al viento.

Hay una cadena que amarra
con invisibles eslabones
la sombra de todos los cuerpos:
por eso el que vende su sombra
vende lo tuyo con lo suyo.

EL TARDÍO

Que se sepa por el transcurso
del lento día de mi vida
que llegué tarde a todas partes:

sólo las sillas me esperaban

(y las olas negras del mar).

Este siglo estaba vacío.

And so, I came to be what I am:

the most parceled heart.

It is known that your heart and what sustains it
are not yours alone:
we presume it's not necessary
to keep kindness in one's pockets:
your sadness begets sadness.

Your roof belongs to the wind.

There is a chain that moors
with invisible links
the shadows of all bodies:
so he who sells his shadow
sells yours as well as his own.

THE LATECOMER

Let it be known that by the course
of the slow day of my life
I arrived late everywhere:

for me, only the chairs waited

(and the black waves of the sea).

This century was empty.

Estaban haciendo las ruedas
de un carruaje de terciopelo.
Para un navío que nacía
se necesitaban adioses.

Las locomotoras aún
tenían sueños de la selva,
se derramaban por los rieles
como cascadas de caimanes
y así la tierra poco a poco
llegó a ser una copa de humo.

Caballos en la amanecida
con los hocicos vaporosos
y las monturas mojadas.
Ah, que galopen como yo,
les pido a los claros poetas,
sobre cinco leguas de barro!

Que se levanten en el frío
(el mundo atónito del alba,
los manzanos llenos de lluvia)
y ensillen en aquel silencio
y galopen hacia la luna!

Un recuerdo

Recuerdo en medio de un trigal
una amapola morada
aún más sedosa que la seda

They were making the wheels
of a velvet carriage.
For any ship being born
farewells were needed.

The locomotives still
dreamed of the forest,
they spilled over the rails
like cascades of caimans
and thus, little by little, the earth
became a goblet of smoke.

Horses at daybreak
with noses steaming
and damp saddles.
Ah, would they gallop as I do?
I ask of the shining poets,
over five leagues of mud.

That they might rise in the cold
(the world astonished by dawn,
the apple trees filled with rain)
and saddle up in that silence
and gallop toward the moon!

A MEMORY

I remember in the middle of a wheat field
a purple poppy
more silken than silk

y con aroma de serpiente.
Lo demás era la aspereza
del trigo cortado y dorado.

Yo me enlacé más de una vez
al lado de una trilladora
con una manzana campestre
de sexo abierto y repentino
y quedó en la paja temblando
un olor a semen y a luna.

El mismo

Me costó mucho envejecer,
acaricié la primavera
como a un mueble recién comprado,
de madera olorosa y lisa,
y en sus cajones escondidos
acumulé la miel salvaje.

Por eso sonó la campana
llevándose a todos los muertos
sin que la oyera mi razón:
uno se acostumbra a su piel,
a su nariz, a su hermosura,
hasta que de tantos veranos
se muere el sol en su brasero.

Mirando el saludo del mar
o su insistencia en el tormento
me quedé volando en la orilla

with the fragrance of a serpent.
All the rest was the ruggedness
of the wheat, cut and golden.

More than once I got myself entangled
alongside a thresher
with a country apple
of open and sudden sex,
and in the shuddering straw lingered
the scent of semen and moon.

SAME ONE

It cost me a lot to grow old—
I caressed spring
as though it were furniture, newly purchased,
made of smooth and fragrant wood,
and in its hidden drawers
I collected wild honey.

That is why the bell rang out
carrying away all the dead
without my mind hearing its appeal:
one grows used to his skin,
his nose, his good looks,
until from so many summers
the sun dies in his bonfire.

Watching the sea's greeting
or its insistence on torment
I remained flying along the shore

o sentado sobre las olas
y guardo de este aprendizaje
un aroma verde y amargo
que acompaña mis movimientos.

MARES

La razón de la desventura
aprendí en la escuela del agua.
El mar es un planeta herido
y la ruptura es su grandeza:
cayó esta estrella en nuestras manos:
desde la torre de la sal
se desprendió su patrimonio
de sombra activa y luz furiosa.

No se ha casado con la tierra.

No lo entendemos todavía.

EL OCIOSO

Que me perdone el enemigo
si perdí tanto tiempo hablando
con arenas y minerales:
no tuve ninguna razón
pero aprendí mucho silencio.

or sitting on the waves,
and I carry from this apprenticeship
a green and bitter smell
that accompanies my every move.

SEAS

I learned the why of misfortune
in the school of water.
The sea is a wounded planet
and the breaking is its greatness:
this star fell into our hands:
from the tower of salt
scatters its heritage
of living shadow and furious light.

It has not married the earth.

We still do not understand it.

THE IDLER

May the enemy forgive me
if I wasted too much time speaking
with sands and minerals:
I had no real reason
but I learned a lot about silence.

Me gusta tocar y gastar
estas piedras de cada día:
el granito color de mosca
que se desgrana y desparrama
en los litorales de Chile.
Nadie sabe cómo llegaron
estas estatuas a la costa.

Si bien adoro el resplandor
de las fosfóricas bengalas,
los castillos de fuego fatuo,
amo en la piedra el corazón,
el fuego que allí se detuvo:
su intransigente permanencia.

1968

La hora de Praga me cayó
como una piedra en la cabeza,
era inestable mi destino,
un momento de oscuridad
como el de un túnel en un viaje
y ahora a fuerza de entender
no llegar a comprender nada:
cuando debíamos cantar
hay que golpear en un sarcófago
y lo terrible es que te oigan
y que te invite el ataúd.

Por qué entre tantas alegrías
que se construyeron sangrando

I like to touch and waste
these stones of each day:
granite the color of flies
which disintegrates and scatters
along the littoral of Chile.
No one knows how these statues
got here, to the coast.

Even though I adore the brilliance
of matchlike Bengalese lights,
the castles of fatuous fire,
I love the heart in the stone,
the fire that stopped there:
its unyielding permanence.

1968

The hour of Prague fell
on my head like a stone,
my destiny was unsteady,
a moment of darkness
as in a tunnel on a journey
and now, trying to understand,
understanding nothing:
whenever we should be singing
we instead must knock upon a sarcophagus,
and how awful it is that they hear you
and that the coffin invites you.

Why among so many joys
that were built with blood

sobre la nieve salpicada
por las heridas de los muertos
y cuando ya el sol olvidó
las cicatrices de la nieve
llega el miedo y abre la puerta
para que regrese el silencio?

Yo reclamo a la edad que viene
que juzgue mi padecimiento,
la compañía que mantuve
a pesar de tantos errores.
Sufrí, sufrimos sin mostrar,
sin mostrar sino la esperanza.

Sufrimos de no defender
la flor que se nos amputaba
para salvar el árbol rojo
que necesita crecimiento.

Fue fácil para el adversario
echar vinagre por la grieta
y no fue fácil definir
y fue más difícil callar.
Pido perdón para este ciego
que veía y que no veía.

Se cierran las puertas del siglo
sobre los mismos insepultos
y otra vez llamarán en vano
y nos iremos sin oír,
pensando en el árbol más grande,
en los espacios de la dicha.

spattered across the snow
from the wounds of the dead,
why, now that the sun forgot
the scars of the snow,
does fear arrive and the door open
so that silence may return?

I appeal to the coming age
to judge my suffering,
the company I kept
despite so many mistakes.
I suffered, we suffered quietly,
revealing only our hope.

We suffered from not defending
the flower we amputated
to save the red tree
that needs to keep growing.

It was easy for the adversary
to pour vinegar over the cut
and it was not easy to define
and was harder still to silence.
I ask forgiveness for this blind man
who saw and who didn't see.

The doors of the century close
on the same ones still left unburied
and again they will call in vain
and we will leave without hearing,
pondering the greater tree,
in the places of our joy.

No tiene remedio el que sufre
para matar el sufrimiento.

EL TIEMPO EN LA VIDA

No me alimentan los recuerdos
y salto a la vida evidente
moviendo el yeso de este siglo
y el zapato de cada día
sufriendo sin cruz el tormento
de ser el más crucificado,
hecho trizas bajo las ruedas
del falso siglo victorioso.

Valía la pena cantar
cuando en España los puñales
dejaron un millón de ausentes,
cuando allí murió la verdad?
La despeñaron al osario
y se tejieron las banderas
con el silencio de los muertos.

Yo vuelvo al tema desangrado
como un general del olvido
que sigue viendo su derrota:
no sólo los muertos murieron
en los brazos de la batalla,
en la prisión, en el castigo,
en las estepas del destierro,
sino que a nosotros también,

Hopeless is he who suffers
to kill suffering.

TIME IN THE LIFE

Memories do not nourish me,
and I embark on the life before me
moving the plaster of this century
and the shoe of each day,
suffering without a cross the torment
of being the one most crucified,
torn to shreds under the wheels
of the false, victorious century.

Was it worthwhile to sing
when in Spain the daggers
left a million missing,
when there, the truth died out?
They hurled it into the boneyard
and wove the flags
with the silence of the dead.

I return to the theme bled dry
like a general of forgetting
who goes reviewing his defeat:
not only did the dead die
in the arms of battle,
in the prison, in punishment,
on the steppes of exile,
but we also,

a los que vivimos aún,
ya se sabe que nos mataron.

OTRA VEZ

Íbamos recién resurrectos
buscando otra vez la ambrosía,
buscando la vida lineal,
la limpieza de los rectángulos,
la geometría sin recodos:
otra vez tuvieron aroma
las mujeres y los antílopes,
los alhelíes, las campanas,
las gotas del mar en invierno,
y otra vez la muerte en Europa
nos naufragó sobre la sangre.

Ardieron en sus madrigueras
aquellos lobos circunspectos
y la presencia del incendio
se fue de país a país:
la noche cruzaba el terror
nacido en las cervecerías
y con la cruz de la crueldad
cruzó como un escalofrío
el bigotito del frenético
sobre las vértebras del mundo.
Nadie podía detener
su locomotora sangrienta.

those of us still alive:
it is well known, they killed us.

ONCE AGAIN

We went, recently resurrected,
again seeking the ambrosia,
seeking the linear life,
the cleanness of rectangles,
the geometry without twists:
the women and the antelopes
again gave off their scents,
the gillyflowers, the bells,
the drops of the sea in winter,
and again the dying in Europe
shipwrecked us on blood.

They burned in their burrows,
those cautious wolves,
and the presence of the fire
spread from country to country:
the night was crossing terror
born in the breweries,
and with the cross of cruelty
the frenetic's small mustache
crossed like a shiver
over the vertebrae of the world.
No one could stop
his bloody locomotive.

Ya se fatigó la memoria
de contar a todos los muertos:
muertos de encías destrozadas
porque tenían dientes de oro,
muertos de cabello cortado
para desnudarlos de todo,
muertos que cavaron la fosa
en la que fueron sepultados,
muertos que buscan su cabeza
entre las manos del verdugo,
muertos de un golpe de aire rojo
en la sombra del bombardeo.

Oh cuánto dispuso la muerte
en las praderas de este siglo:
se conoce que la Cabrona
quería jugar con nosotros
y nos dejó un planeta roto
atiborrado de esqueletos
con llanuras exterminadas
y con ciudades retorcidas,
desdentadas por el incendio,
ciudades negras y vacías
con calles que sólo sustentan
en silencio y las quemaduras.

LA CENIZA

Ésta es la edad de la ceniza.
Ceniza de niños quemados,
de ensayos fríos del infierno,

Memory soon grew tired
from counting all the dead:
the dead of gums smashed
for their teeth filled with gold,
the dead with hair shaved
so as to strip them of everything,
the dead who dug the grave
in which they were buried,
the deceased who sought their own head
between the hands of the executioner,
the dead of a gust of red air
in the shadow of the bombing.

Oh, death laid down so many
in the meadows of this century:
it is well known that she, Death,
wanted to wreak havoc on us,
and left us a broken planet
jammed with skeletons,
with exterminated plains
and with twisted cities,
toothless by fire,
black and empty cities
with streets that sustain only
the silence and the burns.

THE ASHES

This is the age of ashes.
Ashes of burned children,
of cold trials of hell,

cenizas de ojos que lloraron
sin saber de qué se trataba
antes de que los calcinaran,
cenizas de vírgenes góticas
y ventanitas alambradas,
cenizas de roncas bodegas,
desmoronados almacenes,
cenizas de manos insignes.
Y para contar y cerrar
el capítulo ceniciento
en la victoria de Berlín,
las cenizas del asesino
sobre su propio cenicero.

El culto (I)

Ay qué pasión la que cantaba
entre la sangre y la esperanza:
el mundo quería nacer
después de morir tantas veces:
los ojos no tenían lágrimas
después de haber llorado tanto.

No había nada en las arterias,
todo se había desangrado
y sin embargo se arregló
otra vez el pecho del hombre.
Se levantaron las ciudades,
fueron al mar los marineros,
tuvieron niños las escuelas,
y los pájaros, en el bosque,

ashes of eyes that cried
not knowing what was happening
before they were turned to ash,
ashes of gothic virgins
and small wire windows,
ashes of raucous cellars,
crumbling shops,
ashes of famous hands.
And to recount and close
the ashen chapter
in the victory of Berlin,
the ashes of the murderer
in his own ashtray.

THE WORSHIP (I)

Oh, what passion, which was singing
between blood and hope:
the world wanted to be born
after dying so many times:
its eyes held no tears
after so much weeping.

Nothing was left in its arteries,
everything had bled out,
though again did survive
the heart of mankind.
The cities rose up,
the sailors went to sea,
the schools received children,
and the birds, in the woods,

pusieron sus huevos fragantes
sobre los árboles quemados.

Pero fue duro renovar
la sonrisa de la esperanza:
se plantaba en algunos rostros
y se les caía a la calle
y en verdad pareció imposible
rellenar de nuevo la tierra
con tantos huecos que dejó
la dentellada del desastre.

Y cuando ya crecieron las flores,
las cinerarias del olvido,
un hombre volvió de Siberia
y recomenzó la desdicha.

Y si las manos de la guerra,
las terribles manos del odio
nos hundieron de no creer,
de no comprender la razón,
de no conocer la locura,
siempre fue ajena aquella culpa
y ahora sin comprender nada
y sin conocer la verdad
nos pegamos en las paredes
de los errores y dolores
que partían desde nosotros
y estos tormentos otra vez
se acumularon en mi alma.

laid their fragrant eggs
in the burnt trees.

But it was hard to restore
the smile of hope:
it remained on some faces
and fell from them in the street,
and in truth it seemed impossible
to again fill in the earth,
so many hollows were left
by the snapping jaw of disaster.

And soon when the flowers grew,
the cinerarias of forgetting,
a man returned from Siberia
and renewed the misfortune.

And if by the hands of war,
the terrible hands of hate,
we sank for not wanting to believe,
for not understanding the reason,
for not recognizing the madness,
it was always someone else's fault
and now not understanding anything
and not knowing the truth
we pin ourselves against the walls
of the mistakes and sorrows
that flowed from us,
and again these torments
collected in my soul.

II

La marejada se llevó
todos los cercos de la orilla:
tal vez era el sueño del mar,
la dinamita del abismo:
la verdad es que no hay palabras
tan duras como el oleaje,
ni hay tantos dientes en el mundo
como en la cólera marina.

Cuando se enrolla la diadema
del mar y arrecian sus escudos
y las torres se levantaron,
cuando galopa con los pies
de mil millones de caballos
y la cabeza enfurecida
pega en la piedra del relámpago,
agárrate a Dios, alma mía,
dice el pescador pequeñito
golpeándose el pecho mojado
para morir sin agonía.

Crispado mar, tortuga amarga,
panoplia del asesinato,
diapasón de la guerra a muerte,
piano de dientes carniceros,
hoy derribaste mis defensas
con un pétalo de tu furia

II

The rolling wave carried away
all the fences of the shore:
perhaps it was the sea's dream,
the dynamite of the abyss:
the truth is that there are no words
as tough as the surf,
nor are there as many teeth in the world
as in the sea's fury.

When the diadem of the sea
entangles and its shields intensify
and the towers rose up,
when it gallops with the feet
of a thousand million horses
and the enraged head
sticks to the stone of lightning,
cling to God, my soul,
the little fisherman says,
beating his wet chest
so as to die a painless death.

Contorted sea, bitter turtle,
murderous array,
octave of war tuned to death,
piano of carnivorous teeth,
today you tore down my defenses
with a petal of your fury,

y como un ave crepitante
cantabas en los arrecifes.

Aquí está el mar, dicen los ojos,
pero hay que esperar una vida
para vivirlo hasta la muerte
y te premia una tempestad
con cuatro gotas de granito.

En la Punta del Trueno anduve
recogiendo sal en el rostro
y del océano, en la boca
el corazón huracanado:
lo vi estallar hasta el cenit,
morder el cielo y escupirlo.

En cada ráfaga llevaba
el armamento de una guerra,
todas las lágrimas del mundo
y un tren repleto de leones,
pero no era bastante aún
y derribaba lo que hacía
despeñando sobre la piedra
una lluvia de estatuas frías.

Oh firmamento del revés,
oh estrellas hirvientes del agua,
oh marejada del rencor,
dije, mirando la hermosura
de todo el mar desordenado
en una batalla campal
contra mi patria sacudida

and like a crackling bird
you sang on the reefs.

Here is the sea, say the eyes,
but one must wait a lifetime
to live it unto death,
and it awards you a storm
with four drops of granite.

On Punta del Trueno I walked
collecting salt on my face—
and from the ocean, in my mouth
the hurricane heart:
I saw it explode high as the sky,
biting the sky and spitting it out.

In each gust arrived
the armaments of a war,
the tears of the whole world
and a train packed with lions,
but that still was not enough
and it demolished everything in its path,
hurling onto the stone
a rain of cold statues.

Oh, firmament of the slap,
oh, seething stars of water,
oh, wave of rancor,
said I, watching the beauty
of the whole sea in disarray,
in a pitched battle
against my motherland, shaken

por un temblor inexorable
y los designios de la espuma.

ÉPOCA

Aquí no descansa un pasado
que llamé con una campana
para que despierten las cosas
y me rodeen los anillos
que se apartaron de los dedos
obedeciendo a la muerte:

no quiero reconstituir
ni las manos ni los dolores:

después de todo morirá
de una vez por todas tal vez
este siglo de la agonía
que nos enseñó a asesinar
y a morir de sobrevivientes.

EL PELIGRO

Sí, nos dijeron: No resbalen
en los salones encerados
ni en barro ni en nieve ni en lluvia.
Muy bien, dijimos, a seguir
sin resbalar en el invierno.

by an inexorable tremor
and the intentions of the foam.

EPOCH

Here it does not rest, a past
I summoned with a bell
so that things awaken
and the rings gather around me,
which have separated from fingers
obeying death:

I did not want to reconstruct
the hands or the sadnesses:

after everything,
once and for all
shall die this century of agony
that taught us to assassinate
and to die of survival.

THE DANGER

Yes, they told us: do not slip
in the waxed drawing rooms
or in the mud or the snow or the rain.
Very well, we said, and carried on
without slipping in winter.

Pero qué sucedió? Sentimos
bajo los pies algo que huía
y que nos hacía caer.

Era la sangre de este siglo.

Bajó de las secretarías,
de los ventisqueros saqueados,
del mármol de las escaleras
y cruzó el campo, la ciudad,
las redacciones, los teatros,
los almacenes de ceniza,
las rejas de los coroneles:
la sangre cubría las zanjas
y saltaba de guerra en guerra
sobre millones de ojos muertos
que sólo miraban la sangre.

Esto pasó. Yo lo atestiguo.

Ustedes vivirán tal vez
resbalando sólo en la nieve.

A mí me tocó este dolor
de resbalar sobre la sangre.

SEPAN LO SEPAN LO SEPAN

Ay la mentira que vivimos
fue el pan nuestro de cada día.
Señores del siglo veintiuno

So then, what happened? Under our feet
we felt something was fleeing
and was making us fall.

It was the blood of this century.

It was shed by secretaries,
by plundering glaciers,
by the marble of the stairs,
and it spread through the country, the city,
the publishers, the theaters,
the stores of ash,
the grates of the colonels:
blood filled the trenches,
leaping from war to war
over millions of dead eyes
that saw nothing but blood.

This happened. I bear witness.

You perhaps lived
slipping only on the snow.

As for me, it was the sorrow
of slipping on the blood.

KNOW IT KNOW IT KNOW IT

Oh, the lie that we lived
became our daily bread.
What we, lords of the twenty-first

es necesario que se sepa
lo que nosotros no supimos,
que se vea el contra y el por,
porque no lo vimos nosotros,
y que no coma nadie más
el alimento mentiroso
que en nuestro tiempo nos nutría.

Fue el siglo comunicativo
de las incomunicaciones:
los cables debajo del mar
fueron a veces verdaderos
cuando la mentira llegó
a tener mayor latitud
y longitudes que el océano:
los lenguajes se acostumbraron
a aderezar el disimulo,
a sugerir las amenazas,
y las largas lenguas del cable
enrollaron como serpientes
el mentidero colosal
hasta que todos compartimos
la batalla de la mentira
y después de mentir corriendo
salimos mintiendo a matar,
llegamos mintiendo a morir.

Mentíamos con los amigos
en la tristeza o el silencio
y el enemigo nos mintió
con la boca llena de odio.

century, did not know
must be known,
must be seen, the dissent and the why,
because we did not see,
so that no one else consumes
the food of lies
that in our time sustained us.

It was the century of communicating
failed communications:
the cables under the sea
were sometimes truthful
when the lie came
to have greater latitude
and longitude than the ocean:
the languages grew accustomed
to cooking the cover-up,
to insinuating threats,
and the long tongues of cable
coiled like serpents
in the colossal calumny,
until we all shared in
the battle of the lie,
and after lying on the run
lying we went out to kill,
and lying we met death.

We lied to our friends
in the sadness or the silence,
and the enemy lied to us
with a mouthful of hate.

Fue la edad fría de la guerra.

Le edad tranquila del odio.

Una bomba de cuando en cuando
quemaba el alma de Vietnam.

Y Dios metido en su escondite
acechaba como una araña
a los remotos provincianos
que con soñolienta pasión
caían en el adulterio.

LAS GUERRAS

Ven acá, sombrero caído,
zapato quemado, juguete,
o montón póstumo de anteojos,
o bien, hombre, mujer, ciudad,
levántense de la ceniza
hasta esta página cansada,
destituida por el llanto.

Ven, nieve negra, soledad
de la injusticia siberiana,
restos raídos del dolor,
cuando se perdieron los vínculos
y se abrumó sobre los justos
la noche sin explicaciones.

It was the cold age of war.

It was the quiet age of hate.

From time to time a bomb
burned the soul of Vietnam.

And God, secure in his hiding place,
like a spider lay in wait
for the distant peasants
who with sleepy passion
fell in adultery.

THE WARS

Come here, fallen hat,
burnt shoe, toy,
or posthumous pile of eyeglasses
or else man, woman, city,
rise from the ash
as far as this weary page,
deprived by the weeping.

Come, black snow, solitude
of Siberian injustice,
frayed remains of pain
when close ties were lost
and the fog of the inexplicable night
overtook the righteous.

Muñeca del Asia quemada
por los aéreos asesinos,
presenta tus ojos vacíos
sin la cintura de la niña
que te abandonó cuando ardía
bajo los muros incendiados
o en la muerte del arrozal.

Objetos que quedaron solos
cerca de los asesinados
de aquel tiempo en que yo viví
avergonzado por la muerte
de los otros que no vivieron.

De ver la ropa tendida
a secar en el sol brillante
recuerdo las piernas que faltan,
los brazos que no las llenaron,
partes sexuales humilladas
y corazones demolidos.

Un siglo de zapaterías
llenó de zapatos el mundo
mientras cercenaban los pies
o por la nieve o por el fuego
o por el gas o por el hacha!

A veces me quedo agachado
de tanto que pesa en mi espalda
la repetición de castigo:
me costó aprender a morir
con cada muerte incomprensible
y llevar los remordimientos

Doll of Asia torched
by the airborne assassins,
show your empty eyes
without the waist of the child
who abandoned you as she flamed
beneath the burned-out walls
or in the death of the rice paddy.

Objects that remained alone
beside those murdered
in that time when I lived
shamed by the death
of those who did not live.

Seeing clothes hung out
to dry in the bright sunshine
I remember the legs that are missing,
the arms that no longer fulfill them,
humiliated sexual parts
and demolished hearts.

A century with shoe shops
filled the world with shoes
while feet were cut off
by snow or by fire,
by gas or by ax!

At times I remain bowed
by all that weighs on my back,
the repeated punishment:
it took a lot for me to learn to die
with each incomprehensible death
and to bear the remorse

del criminal innecesario:
porque después de la crueldad
y aun después de la venganza
no fuimos tal vez inocentes
puesto que seguimos viviendo
cuando mataban a los otros.

Tal vez les robamos la vida
a nuestros hermanos mejores.

LOS DESAPARECIDOS

Lumumba desaparecido,
pregunto, dónde está Ben Bella?
Ben Barka desapareció.

Y así este siglo pululado
por los diestros y los siniestros
ladrones de hombres, usurpantes,
secuestradores y asesinos.

Lumumba va con su razón,
su deslumbrante geometría
por las nubes de la tortura
entregado a los sanguinarios.

África amarga, dónde están
sus delgadas manos morenas?
Cómo entregaste a los verdugos
la flor negra de tu derecho?

of the wantonly criminal:
because after the cruelty
and even after the vengeance
perhaps we were not so innocent
given that we went on with our lives
as they were killing the others.

Perhaps we rob our better brothers
of their lives.

The Missing

The missing Lumumba,
and I ask, where is Ben Bella?
Ben Barka has disappeared.

And thus this century swarmed
with the clever and the sinister—
thieves of men, usurpers,
kidnappers and murderers.

Lumumba passes with rationality,
his dazzling geometry
among the clouds of torture,
given over to the bloodthirsty.

Bitter Africa, where are
your thin brown hands?
How did you hand over to the executioners
the black flower of your birthright?

Ben Barka en medio de París
condenado a morir a oscuras
por monarquías y burdeles,
crucificado en el silencio
de esta época de agonía!

Ben Bella que la ira llevó
en una oscura ola callada
hacia el secreto, y no volvió
de la eternidad de la arena.

Yo prefiero el ruido escarlata
de las ametralladoras
en el infierno de Chicago
de los hombres sin Dios ni ley,
a estos guantes que se movieron
sin manos, para estrangular,
a estas cabezas sin mirada
que buscan en la noche cruel
corazones de héroes perdidos.

O silencio! Oh terror! Adiós!

No queda nada, ya lavaron
las gradas del crimen. Se fueron.

Fueron secretas las condenas
y los verdugos invisibles.

A nosotros nos tocó ver
en vez de la luna en la noche
paseando el cielo como un astro
la dentadura de la muerte.

Ben Barka in the middle of Paris
condemned to die in the dark
by monarchies and brothels,
crucified in the silence
of this age of agony!

Ben Bella, who was borne
toward the secret by a dark silent wave
that never returned
from the eternity of the sand.

I prefer the scarlet racket
of machine guns
in the hell of Chicago,
of the men without God or law,
to these gloves that moved
without hands and set out to strangle,
to these faces with no expression
that seek in the cruel night
hearts of lost heroes.

Oh silence! Oh terror! Goodbye!

Nothing remains, they already scrubbed
the steps of the crime. They left.

The convictions were secret
and the executioners invisible.

It was upon us to see
instead of the moon at night
riding the sky like a star—
the teeth of death.

No nos volvamos a medir
con la atmósfera delicada,
ella depende de una gota,
de una nube, de un alhelí:
tú pestañeas y en el acto
el cielo cambia de camisa.

Entremos a nosotros mismos,
a tu zaguán, a tu almanaque,
y sobre todo a la bodega
donde guardas los muebles rotos
y las lámparas apagadas,
más aún, las tristes rupturas
que se escondieron en silencio,
los secretos que se pudrieron,
las llaves tiradas al mar.

Bajemos al piso de abajo
y destapemos el infierno,
siempre de allí te están llamando
en idiomas que nadie entiende,
salvo tú mismo sólo a veces
porque nunca quieres oír
cuando te llaman desde adentro,
desde el recuerdo inoxidable.

Let us not go back to measure
the tender atmosphere,
she depends on one drop,
on one cloud, on a gillyflower:
you blink and in the act
the sky changes its shirt.

Let us enter ourselves,
your hall, your almanac,
and above all the warehouse
where you keep the broken furniture
and the extinguished lamps,
even more, the sad fractures
that were hidden in silence,
the secrets that rotted,
the keys thrown to the sea.

Let us descend to the lower floor
and let us uncover hell,
from there, always, they call you
in languages that no one knows,
except for you, at certain times only,
because you never want to hear
when they call you from within,
from your stainless memory.

El sol nace de su semilla
a su esplendor obligatorio,
lava con luz el universo,
se acuesta a morir cada día
bajo las sábanas oscuras
de la noche germinadora
y para nacer otra vez
deja su huevo en el rocío.

Pido que mi resurrección
también sea reproductiva,
sea solar y delicada,
pero necesito dormir
en las sábanas de la luna
procreando modestamente
mis propias substancias terrestres.

Quiero extenderme en el vacío
desinteresado del viento
y propagarme sin descanso
en los cuarenta continentes,
nacer en formas anteriores,
ser camello, ser codorniz,
ser campanario en movimiento,
hoja del agua, gota de árbol,
araña, ballena del cielo
o novelista tempestuoso.

Ya sé que mi inmovilidad
es la garantía invisible
de todo el establecimiento:

The sun is born of its seed
to its obligatory brilliance,
it washes the universe with light,
lies down each day to die
under the dark sheets
of the budding night,
and to be born again
it leaves its egg in the dew.

I ask that my resurrection
also be reproductive,
solar and delicate,
but I need to sleep
in sheets of moonlight
modestly conceiving
my own earthly substances.

I want to spread out in the emptiness
indifferent to the wind
and ceaselessly beget myself
on the forty continents,
to be born in earlier forms,
to be camel, to be quail,
to be belfry in motion,
leaf of the water, drop of tree,
spider, whale of the sky
or stormy novelist.

I now see that my immobility
is what invisibly guarantees
the entire establishment:

si cambiamos de zoología
no nos admiten en el cielo.

Por eso sentado en mi piedra
veo girar sobre mis sueños
los helicópteros que vuelven
de sus estrellas diminutas
y no necesito contarlos,
siempre hay algunos en exceso,
sobre todo en la primavera.

Y si me voy por los caminos
recurro al aroma olvidado
de una rosa deshabitada,
de una fragancia que perdí
como se extravía la sombra:
me quedé sin aquel amor
desnudo en medio de la calle.

if we at all change zoology
they will not admit us to heaven.

For that reason, seated on my stone,
I see whirling over my dreams
the helicopters as they return
from their diminutive stars,
and I do not need to count them,
there are always extra,
above everything in spring.

And if I leave on the roads
I turn to the forgotten aroma
of an uninhabited rose,
of a fragrance that I lost
like a shadow loses its way:
I remained with no love at all,
naked in the middle of the street.

III

Florece este día de invierno
con una sola rosa muerta,
la noche prepara su nave,
caen los pétalos del cielo
y sin rumbo vuelve la vida
a recogerse en una copa.

Yo no sé decir de otro modo:
la noche negra, el día rojo,
y recibo las estaciones
con cortesía de poeta:
espero puntual la llegada
de las verbales golondrinas
y monto una guardia de acero
frente a las puertas del otoño.

Por eso el invierno imprevisto
me sobrecoge en su accidente
como el humo desalentado
del recuerdo de una batalla:
no es la palabra *padecer*,
no es *escarmiento*, no es *desdicha*,
es como un sonido en la selva,
como un tambor bajo la lluvia.
Lo cierto es que cambia mi tema
con el color de la mañana.

III

This winter day blooms
with a single dead rose,
the night prepares its ship,
the petals of the sky fall,
and lacking direction life returns
to gather itself in a wineglass.

I don't know how else to say it:
the black night, the red day,
and I greet each station
with the courtesy of a poet:
punctual, I await the arrival
of the chattering swallows
and I mount a steely guard
facing the doors of autumn.

That is why unexpected winter
startles me with its accident
like disheartened smoke
of the memory of a battle:
it is not the word *suffer,*
not *lesson,* not *misfortune,*
it is like a sound in the forest,
like a drum in the rain.
What's certain is, my theme changes
with the color of morning.

CAYENDO

Yo te llamo, rosa de leche,
duplicada paloma de agua,
ven desde aquella primavera
a resucitar en las sábanas,
a encender detrás del invierno
el sol erótico del día.

Hoy en mi propia circunstancia
soy un desnudo peregrino
viajando a la iglesia del mar:
crucé las piedras saladas,
seguí el discurso de los ríos
y me senté junto a la hoguera
sin saber que era mi destino.

Sobreviviente de la sal,
de las piedras y de las llamas,
sigo cruzando las regiones
sosteniéndome en mis dolores,
enamorado de mi sombra.
Por eso no por mucho andar
llego a alejarme de mí mismo.

Es este día mentiroso
de falsa luz encapotada,
lo que me puso macilento:
me caigo en el tiempo del pozo
y después de nadar debajo
de la inexacta primavera
salgo a la luz en cualquier parte

FALLING

I call to you, rose of milk,
twin dove of water,
come from that spring
and return to life between the sheets,
kindle behind the winter
the erotic sun of the day.

Today, given my situation,
I am a naked pilgrim
traveling to the church of the sea:
I crossed the salt-encrusted stones,
I followed the discourse of rivers,
and I felt myself joined to the bonfire
not knowing what my destiny would be.

Surviving the salt,
the stones and the flames,
I go on crossing the regions
sustaining me in my sadness,
enamored of my own shadow.
That is why, however little I walk,
I find myself farther from myself.

It is this deceiving day,
of false, cloudy light,
that made me so pale:
I fall into the time of the well,
and after swimming beneath
the inexact spring
I come out into the light, no matter where,

con el mismo sombrero gris
tocando la misma guitarra.

TAL VEZ

Es cuerdo el hombre que voltea
y parpadeando en el alambre
cambia de piel y paladar
buscando el sol o el equilibrio.
(La astucia cambia de color
y el conservador no conserva
sino las máscaras que usó
ya convertidas en ceniza.)

DIABLITOS

He visto cómo preparaba
su condición el oportuno,
su coartada el arribista,
sus redes la rica barata,
sus inclusiones el poeta.

Yo jugué con el papel limpio
frente a la luz todos los días.

Yo soy obrero pescador
de versos vivos y mojados
que siguen saltando en mis venas.

with the same gray hat,
playing the same guitar.

PERHAPS

The man is wise who swings
and blinking on the wire
changes skin and palate,
seeking the sun and balance.
(Cleverness changes color
and the conservative conserves nothing
but the masks he wore,
already turned to ash.)

LITTLE DEVILS

I have seen how the rich one
would prepare his character,
the social climber his alibi,
the gold digger her nets,
the poet his inclusions.

I played with blank paper,
each day facing the light.

I am a working fisher
of verses, living and wet,
that go leaping in my veins.

Nunca supe hacer otra cosa
ni supe urdir los menesteres
del intrínseco jactancioso
o del perverso intrigador,
y no es propaganda del bien
lo que estoy diciendo en mi canto:
sino que no lo supe hacer,
y les pido excusas a todos:
déjenme solo con el mar:
yo nací para pocos peces.

SÍ, SEÑOR

Yo nací para pocos peces,
para la infinita frescura
de cada gota del trabajo,
y el rosario que se fue hilando,
la escama clara y repetida.

Me declararon transparente
y así sin darme cuenta yo
llegué a hablar como todo el mundo.

CAMINOS

Encontré un hombre en un camión
que me entretuvo conversando
en el camión que manejaba

I never knew how to make anything else
or knew how to curb the needs
of the natural braggart
or of the man of intrigue,
and this is not propaganda for the good
I am speaking in my song:
I just didn't know how to craft it,
and I apologize to everyone:
leave me alone with the sea:
I was born to small fish.

YES, SIR

I was born for small fish,
for the infinite freshness
of each drop of labor,
and the rosary being spun,
the clear and repeating scale.

They declared me transparent,
so without realizing it, I
came to speak like everybody else.

ROADS

I came across a man in a truck
who entertained me with conversation
in that truck he was driving

entre Osorno y Antofagasta.
La noche de Chile es más larga,
la noche de Chile es eterna,
la noche de la carretera
desenrollada por los faros,
y no termina en parte alguna.
No se sabe dónde comienza
la cinta nocturna de Chile
de estrellas secas en el Norte,
en el Sur de estrellas mojadas.
En la estrecha sombra chilena
sigue el camión intermitente
con el camionero que fuma
junto a los sacos taciturnos
dejando atrás la noche angosta,
redonda como una culebra.
Se llamaba Jesús González
mi amigo del camión de carga.

PAISAJE

Anduve diciéndoles adiós
a muchos distantes, y ahora
me gustaría recoger
el hilo de aquellos adioses,
volver a ver ojos perdidos.

No sé si a todos les conviene
mi melancolía de hoy:
estoy dispuesto a repartirla
en pequeños granos redondos

between Osorno and Antofagasta.
The night of Chile is so very long,
the night of Chile is eternal,
the night of the highway
unfurled by lighthouse beacons,
and nowhere does it end.
It is not known where it begins,
the nocturnal ribbon of Chile,
of dry stars in the North,
in the South of damp stars.
In the thin Chilean shadow
the occasional truck rolls on
with the trucker who smokes,
beside the silent sacks,
leaving behind the narrow night,
round like a snake.
His name was Jesús Gonzáles
my friend of the loaded truck.

COUNTRYSIDE

I walked on, saying goodbye
to so many far away, and now
I would like to gather
the thread of those goodbyes,
to once again see lost eyes.

I am not sure it agrees with everyone,
my melancholy today:
I am ready to divide it up
in small round grains

alrededor del campamento,
en las rodillas del camino.
Quiero ver si crece la pena,
las flores de la incertidumbre,
la indecisión apesarada:
quiero saber de qué color
son las hojas del abandono.

Cuando un día te mira el sol
como un tigre desde su trono
y quiere obligarte a vivir
su condición voluntariosa,
recibo una racha lunática,
me desespero de sombrío,
y cuando menos lo esperaba
me pongo a repartir tristeza.

EL FUEGO

Qué momento tan musical
me dice un río inteligente
al mover junto a mí sus aguas:
él se divierte con las piedras,
sigue cantando su camino,
mientras yo decidido a todo
lo miro con ojos de furia.

Dediquemos a la desdicha
un pensamiento vaporoso
como la tierra matinal
sucia de lágrimas celestes

all around the camp,
I want to see if grief grows,
the flowers of uncertainty,
the grief-stricken indecision:
I want to know what color
are the leaves of abandonment.

When one day the sun watches you
like a tiger from its throne
and wishes to compel you to live
in its willful state,
I am hit by a gust of madness,
I despair of gloom and doom,
and when I least expect to,
I set about sharing my sadness.

THE FIRE

What a musical moment
a clever river says to me
in its movement tying me to its waters:
he amuses himself with stones,
he follows singing his own road,
while I, resolved to everything,
watch him with furious eyes.

Let us dedicate to misfortune
a misty thought
as the morning earth
dirtied by light blue tears

levanta un árbol de vapor
que desenfoca la mañana:
sufre la luz que iba naciendo,
se amotina la soledad
y ya no se cuenta con nada,
no se ve el cielo ni la tierra
bajo la neblina salobre.

Exageramos este asunto,
dije volviendo a la fogata
que se apagaba en la espesura
y con dos ramas de laurel
se levantó una llama roja
con una castaña en el centro,
y luego se abrió la castaña
enseñándome la lección
de su dulzura aprisionada
y volví a ser un ciudadano
que quiere leer los periódicos.

EL SIGLO MUERE

Treinta y dos años entrarán
trayendo el siglo venidero,
treinta y dos trompetas heroicas,
treinta y dos fuegos derrotados,
y el mundo seguirá tosiendo
envuelto en su sueño y su crimen.

Tan pocas hojas que le faltan
al árbol de las amarguras

raises a tree of mist
that blurs the morning:
the light being born suffers,
the solitude revolts
and now nothing is counted on,
neither sky nor earth can be seen
beneath the brackish mist.

We exaggerate this matter,
Said I, returning to the bonfire
that was dying in the thickness,
and with two branches of laurel
one red flame rose up
with a chestnut at its center,
then the chestnut cracked open
teaching me the lesson
of its imprisoned sweetness,
and I went back to being a citizen
who wants to read the newspapers.

THE CENTURY DIES

Thirty-two years will come
bringing the coming century,
thirty-two heroic trumpets,
thirty-two defeated fires,
and the world will go on coughing,
wrapped in its dream and its crime.

So few leaves are missing
from the tree of bitterness

para los cien años de otoño
que destruyeron el follaje:
lo regaron con sangre blanca,
con sangre negra y amarilla,
y ahora quiere una medalla
en su pechera de sargento
el siglo que cumple cien años
de picotear ojos heridos
con sus herramientas de hierro
y sus garras condecoradas.

Me dice el cemento en la calle,
me canta el pájaro enramado,
me advierte la cárcel nombrando
los justos allí ajusticiados,
me lo declaran mis parientes,
mis intranquilos compañeros,
secretarios de la pobreza:
siguen podridos estos años
parados en medio del tiempo
como los huesos de una res
que devoran los roedores
y salen de la pestilencia
libros escritos por las moscas.

POR QUÉ, SEÑOR?

A los cinco años de este siglo
Estados Unidos cantaba
como una máquina de plata,
susurraba con el sonido

for the hundred years of autumn
that destroyed the foliage:
they watered it with white blood,
with black and yellow blood,
and now it wants a medal
on the breast of its sergeant's uniform,
the century that celebrates one hundred years
of pecking at wounded eyes
with its tools of iron
and its decorated talons.

The concrete in the street says to me,
the bird, decorated with branches, sings to me,
the prison warns me, naming
the righteous executed there,
my relatives declare it,
my worried companions,
secretaries of poverty:
the rotten years continue,
halted in the middle of time
like the bones of a beast
being devoured by rodents,
and what emerges from pestilence
are books written by flies.

WHY, SIR?

Five years into this century
the United States was singing
like a silver machine,
it was whispering with the sound

de un granero que se desgrana,
tenía las manos de Lincoln
y la abundancia de Walt Whitman,
bajaban por el Mississippi
las barcarolas de los negros
y Nueva York era una olla
con un repollo gigantesco.

Dónde está ahora aquella gente?
Y aquella nación qué se hizo?
Lincoln y Whitman qué se hicieron?

Dónde están las nieves de antaño?
Ahora con tantas estrellas
que condecoran su chaleco,
con tantos edificios de oro
y tantas bombas en el puño
y con la sangre que derraman
no los quiere nadie en la tierra:
no son los Estados Unidos,
son los Estados Escupidos.

Sin tener ni por qué ni cuándo
se deshonraron en Vietnam.
Por qué tenían que matar
a los lejanos inocentes
cuando hacen nata los delitos
en los bosillos de Chicago?
Por qué ir tan lejos a matar?
Por qué ir tan lejos a morir?

Primos hermanos por la tierra,
por el espacio y las praderas,

of a granary husked of grain,
it possessed the hands of Lincoln
and the abundance of Walt Whitman,
the barcaroles of the blacks
rolled down the Mississippi,
and New York was a kettle
containing a gigantic cabbage.

Where are those people now?
And the nation that was formed?
Lincoln and Whitman, what became of them?

Where are the snows of yesteryear?
Even now, with so many stars
decorating their waistcoat,
so many edifices of gold,
so many bombs in their fist,
with the blood that they spill,
no one on the earth wants them:
they are not the United States,
they are the States of Spittle.

Without why or when
they dishonored themselves in Vietnam.
Why were they so far from home,
compelled to kill innocents,
while the crimes pour cream
into the pockets of Chicago?
Why go so far to kill?
Why go so far to die?

First cousins on earth,
in space and meadows,

por qué nuestros primos tomaron
los estandartes del asalto
y en despoblado a media noche
entraron a la casa ajena
a romper todos los cristales,
a quemar niños con napalm,
y luego sin gloria ni pena
salir con la cola caída
y los guantes ensangrentados?

EN CUBA

Corrió la luz por estas horas
hacia nuestra tierra dormida
y en un relámpago terrestre
se encendió la estrella de Cuba.

Honor, honor a aquel puñado
de hirsutos héroes en la aurora,
honor a la lumbre primera
del sol latinoamericano:
honor y tambor y loor
a los pájaros de la pólvora
y al perfil de los insurgentes.
Yo vi y canté a los que llegaron
y celebré los edificios
que elevó el amor y el combate,
las reses nuevas que nacieron
y el tumultuoso movimiento
que corre cortando y cantando
azúcar del cañaveral.

why did our cousins raise
the banners of the assault
and at deserted midnight
enter other people's houses
to break all the windowpanes,
to burn children with napalm,
and then without glory or grief
leave with tails between their legs
and with bloodied gloves?

IN CUBA

The light passed through these hours
toward our sleeping earth
and an earthly lightning bolt
lit the star of Cuba.

Honor, honor to that handful
of bearded heroes in the dawn,
honor to the first fiery glow
of the Latin American sun:
honor and beating drum and praise
to the birds of gunpowder
and to the profile of the rebels.
I went and sang those who arrived
and I celebrated the edifices
that love and combat raised,
the new beasts that were born
and the churning movement
that flows, cutting and singing
the sugar of the plantation.

Sepan ustedes, los de ahora,
que conocí el ayer cubano,
los anteayeres de La Habana:
todo era baraja y daiquiri,
blancas y negras se vendían
mientras subía a los balcones
un clamor de bocas amargas
con la serenata del hambre:
yo certifico que era así:
torta podrida, estercolero,
atardecer prostibulario.

Antes que nadie y que ninguno
yo canté la cúbita hazaña,
declaré la gesta en mi libro,
propagué la rosa de fuego
y puso a Cuba en la ventana
mi compañera poesía.
No pretendí halago ni honor,
sino el deber del combatiente.

Cuando todo estaba ganado
se asociaron los escribientes
y acumularon firmadores:
todos ellos se acorralaron
disparando contra mi voz,
contra mi canto cristalino
y mi corazón comunista.

En este siglo la amargura
se ocultó antes y después
de cada espléndida victoria:
fue como un gato que acechara

Know it, you of this day,
the Cuban past I knew,
the days before yesterday in Havana:
everything was playing cards and daiquiris,
white and black women sold themselves
while a clamoring of bitter mouths
climbed to the balconies
in the serenade of hunger:
I swear that it was so:
rotten cake, heap of manure,
evening of the brothel.

Sooner than anyone else and than no one
I sang the cubic feat,
I declared the heroic deed in my book,
I propagated the rose of fire
and it placed Cuba in the window,
my comrade poetry did.
I did not seek flattery or honor
but to fulfill my duty as a fighter.

When all was won
the clerks banded together,
and those who signed grew in number:
all were cornered
shooting at my voice,
at my crystalline song
and my communist heart.

In this century, bitterness
concealed itself before and after
every splendid victory:
it was like a cat that lies in wait

el vuelo más vertiginoso
y restituyera a la jaula
un aletazo moribundo.
Sin embargo el amanecer
se sostuvo y brillaba el cielo.

TRISTEZA EN LA MUERTE DE UN HÉROE

Los que vivimos esta historia,
esta muerte y resurrección
de nuestra esperanza enlutada,
los que escogimos el combate
y vimos crecer las banderas,
supimos que los más callados
fueron nuestros únicos héroes
y que después de las victorias
llegaron los vociferantes
llena la boca de jactancia
y de proezas salivares.

El pueblo movió la cabeza:
y volvió el héroe a su silencio.
Pero el silencio se enlutó
hasta ahogarnos en el luto
cuando moría en las montañas
el fuego ilustre de Guevara.

El comandante terminó
asesinado en un barranco.

for that most spiraling flight
and restores to the cage
a dying wingbeat.
Nevertheless the dawn
won out and the sky lit up.

SADNESS AT THE DEATH OF A HERO

We who lived this history,
this death and resurrection
of our hope dressed in black,
we, whose choice was combat
and who watched the flags grow,
knew that the quietest
were our true heroes,
that after the victories
arrived the windbags,
mouths full of boasts
and exploits of saliva.

The people shook their heads:
and the hero returned to his silence.
But silence mourned
so as to drown us in grief
when in the mountains died
the lustrous fire of Guevara.

The commander ended up
assassinated in a ravine.

Nadie dijo esta boca es mía.
Nadie lloró en los pueblos indios.
Nadie subió a los campanarios.
Nadie levantó los fusiles,
y cobraron la recompensa
aquellos que vino a salvar
el comandante asesinado.

Qué pasó, medita el contrito,
con estos acontecimientos?

Y no se dice la verdad
pero se cubre con papel
esta desdicha de metal.
Recién se abría el derrotero
y cuando llegó la derrota
fue como un hacha que cayó
en la cisterna del silencio.

Bolivia volvió a su rencor,
a sus oxidados gorilas,
a su miseria intransigente,
y como brujos asustados
los sargentos de la deshonra,
los generalitos del crimen,
escondieron con eficiencia
el cadáver del guerrillero
como si el muerto los quemara.

La selva amarga se tragó
los movimientos, los caminos,
y donde pasaron los pies
de la milicia exterminada

No one said this mouth is mine.
No one wept in the indian villages.
No one climbed the bell towers.
No one raised their rifles,
and the reward was claimed
by those whose rescue was the aim
of the assassinated *comandante*.

And what, wondered the remorseful,
could have happened?

But the truth is never spoken,
it is covered with paper,
this calamity of metal.
The route was just opening up
and when defeat arrived
it was like an ax that fell
into the cistern of silence.

Bolivia returned to her rancor,
to her rusted gorillas,
to her stubborn misery,
and like frightened sorcerers
the sergeants of dishonor,
the little generals of crime,
hid with utmost efficiency
the corpse of the guerrilla fighter
as if the dead man might burn them.

The bitter jungle devoured
the movements, the roads,
and where the feet
of the exterminated militia strode

hoy las lianas aconsejaron
una voz verde de raíces
y el ciervo salvaje volvió
al follaje sin estampidos.

today lianas offered advice—
a green voice of roots—
and the wild stag returned
to the leaves free of explosions.

IV

Pero debajo de la alfombra
y más allá del pavimento
entre dos inmóviles olas
un hombre ha sido separado
y debo bajar y mirar
hasta saber de quién se trata.
Que no lo toque nadie aún:
es una lámina, una línea:
una flor guardada en un libro:
una osamenta transparente.

El Oliverio intacto entonces
se reconstituye en mis ojos
con la certeza del cristal,
pero cuanto adelante o calle,
cuanto recoja del silencio,
lo que me cunda en la memoria,
lo que me regale la muerte,
sólo será un pobre vestigio,
una silueta de papel.

Porque el que canto y rememoro
brillaba de vida insurrecta
y compartí su fogonazo,
su ir y venir y revolver,
la burla y la sabiduría,
y codo a codo amanecimos
rompiendo los vidrios del cielo,

IV

But under the carpet
and past the pavement
between two motionless waves,
a man has been split in two,
and I must go down and look closely
to know whom to address.
May no one touch him yet:
he is now a lamina, a line:
a flower pressed in a book:
a transparent skeleton.

Then, the untouched Oliverio
reconstructs himself before my eyes
with the certainty of crystal,
however much he goes forward or grows silent,
however much he takes back of silence,
what he spreads in my memory,
what he gives me in death,
it will be but a poor trace,
a paper silhouette.

Because the one I sing and remember
shined with rebellious life
and I shared his flash,
his going and coming and stirring up,
the taunting and the wisdom,
and elbow to elbow we dawned
breaking the windows of heaven,

subiendo las escalinatas
de palacios desmoronados,
tomando trenes que no existen,
reverberando de salud
en el alba de los lecheros.

Yo era el navegante silvestre
(y se me notaba en la ropa
la oscuridad del archipiélago)
cuando pasó y sobrepasó
las multitudes Oliverio,
sobresaliendo en las aduanas,
solícito en las travesías
(con el plastrón desordenado
en la otoñal investidura),
o cerveceando en la humareda
o espectro de Valparaíso.

En mi telaraña infantil
sucede Oliverio Girondo.

Yo era un mueble de las montañas.

Él, un caballero evidente.
Barbín, barbián, hermano claro,
hermano oscuro, hermano frío,
relampagueando en el ayer
preparabas la luz intrépida,
la invención de los alhelíes,
las sílabas fabulosas
de tu elegante laberinto
y así tu locura de santo
es ornato de la exigencia,

ascending flights of stairs
of corroded palaces,
taking trains that do not exist,
reverberating with health
in the dawn of the milkmen.

I was the wild navigator
(and felt in my clothes
the darkness of the archipelago)
when Oliverio passed or passed beyond
the multitudes,
leaning from the customhouse,
obliging at the crossings
(with his ruffled shirt unruly
in the autumnal investiture),
or drinking beer in the cloud of smoke
or specter of Valparaíso.

In my childlike web
Oliverio Girondo happens.

I was a piece of furniture from the mountains.

He, obviously a gentleman.
Generous, genteel, bright brother,
dark brother, cold brother,
flashing in days past
you readied the intrepid light,
the invention of gillyflowers,
the fabulous syllables
of your elegant labyrinth,
and so your saintly madness
is an ornament of urgency,

como si hubieras dibujado
con una tijera celeste
en la ventana tu retrato
para que lo vean después
con exactitud las gaviotas.

Yo soy el cronista abrumado
por lo que puede suceder
y lo que debo predecir
(sin contar lo que me pasó,
ni lo que a mí me pasaron),
y en este canto pasajero
a Oliverio Girondo canto,
a su insolencia matutina.

Se trata del inolvidable.

De su indeleble puntería:
cuando borró la catedral
y con su risa de corcel
clausuró el turismo de Europa,
reveló el pánico del queso
frente a la francesa golosa
y dirigió al Guadalquivir
el disparo que merecía.

Oh primordial desenfadado!
Hacía tanta falta aquí
tu iconoclasta desenfreno!

Reinaba aún Sully Prud'homme
con su redingote de lilas
y su bonhomía espantosa.

as if you had drawn
with heavenly scissors
your portrait in the window
so they then would view it
with precision, the gulls.

I am the chronicler awed
by what is possible
and what I must predict
(without telling what came to pass,
nor what was passed on to me),
and in this passing song
I sing to Oliverio Girondo,
to his insolence of morning.

It is about the unforgettable.

It's about his indelible aim:
when he erased the cathedral
and with his steedlike laughter
brought to an end European tourism,
he revealed the panic of cheese
facing down the French *gourmande*
and turned upon the Guadalquivir
the fire that it deserved.

O primordially self-assured!
It was so very lacking here,
your iconoclastic nonchalance!

Sully Prud'homme was reigning still
with his overcoat of lilacs
and his frightening geniality.

Hacía falta un argentino
que con las espuelas del tango
rompiera todos los espejos
incluyendo aquel abanico
que fue trizado por un búcaro.

Porque yo, pariente futuro
de la itálica piedra clara
o de Quevedo permanente
o del nacional Aragon,
yo no quiero que espere nadie
la moneda falsa de Europa,
nosotros los pobres américos,
los dilatados en el viento,
los de metales más profundos,
los millonarios de guitarras,
no debemos poner el plato,
no mendiguemos la existencia.

Me gusta Oliverio por eso:
no se fue a vivir a otra parte
y murió junto a su caballo.
Me gustó la razón intrínseca
de su delirio necesario
y el matambre de la amistad
que no termina todavía:
amigo, vamos a encontrarnos
tal vez debajo de la alfombra
o sobre las letras del río
o en el termómetro obelisco
(o en la dirección delicada
del susurro y de la zozobra)

He sorely needed an Argentine
who with his spurs of the tango
would break all the mirrors
and also that fan
shattered by a vase.

Because I, a future relative
of the bright italic stone
or of permanent Quevedo
or of the national Aragon,
do not want anyone to await
the false currency of Europe,
we poor americans,
spread by the wind,
those of the deepest metals,
the millions of the guitar,
we should not set out our own plate,
let us not make a beggar of our existence.

I like Oliverio for this reason:
he did not go away to live somewhere else
and he died in the saddle.
I liked the underlying reason
for his necessary delirium
and the sliced meat of his friendship
that still has not ended:
friend, we are going to find each other
maybe under the carpet
or on the letters of the river
or in the thermometer-like obelisk
(or in the delicate direction
of the whisper and of the shipwreck)

o en las raíces reunidas
bajo la luna de Figari.

Oh energúmeno de la miel,
patriota del espantapájaros,
celebraré, celebré, celebro
lo que cada día serás
y lo Oliverio que serías
compartiendo tu alma conmigo
si la muerte hubiera olvidado
subir una noche, y por qué?
buscando un número, y por qué?
por qué por la calle Suipacha?

De todos los muertos que amé
eres el único viviente.

No me dedico a las cenizas,
te sigo nombrando y creyendo
en tu razón extravagante
cerca de aquí, lejos de aquí,
entre una esquina y una ola
adentro de un día redondo,
en un planeta desangrado
o en el origen de una lágrima.

CAMINANDO CAMINOS

De noche, por las carreteras
de la sequía, piedra y polvo,
tartamudea el carromato.

or in the assembled roots
under the moon of Figari.

O madman of honey,
patriot of the scarecrows,
I will praise, I praised, I praise
what you will be each day
and how, Oliverio, you would be
sharing your soul with me
if death would have forgotten
to climb up one night, and why?
searching for a number, and why?
why up through Suipacha Street?

Of all the dead I loved
you are the only one alive.

I do not dedicate myself to the ashes,
I go on naming and believing
in your extravagant reason
near here, far from here,
between a corner and a wave
inside a round day,
on a planet bled dry,
or in the origin of a tear.

WALKING WALKWAYS

At night, by roads
of the drought, stone, and dust,
the covered wagon stutters.

No pasa nadie por aquí.

El suelo no tiene habitantes
sino la aspereza encendida
por los faros vertiginosos:
es la noche de las espinas,
de los vegetales armados
como caimanes, con cuchillos:
se ven los dientes del alambre
alrededor de los potreros,
los cactus de hostil estatura
como obeliscos espinosos,
la noche seca, y en la sombra
llena de estrellas polvorientas
el nido negro de la aurora
que prepara sin descansar
los horizontes amarillos.

LA SOLEDAD

Cuando llega la soledad
y tú no estás acostumbrado
se destapan cosas cerradas,
baúles que creías muertos,
frascos que asumen la advertencia
de una invariable calavera,
se abren algunas cerraduras,
se destapan ollas del alma.

Pero no nos gusta saber,
no amamos los descubrimientos

No one passes through here.

Nothing calls this land home
other than the ruggedness lit
by vertiginous lighthouses:
it is the night of thorns,
of vegetables armed
like caimans, with knives:
one can see teeth of wire
around the cattle fields,
the cacti of hostile stature
like thorny obelisks,
the dry night, and in the shadow
filled with dusty stars
the black nest of the dawn,
which prepares without rest
the yellow horizons.

SOLITUDE

When solitude arrives
and you are not used to it,
closed things uncover themselves,
trunks that you thought were dead,
small bottles that carry the warning
of an invariable skull,
some locks open,
pots of the soul lift their lids.

But we do not like knowing,
we do not love discovering

de nuestra vieja identidad,
encontrar al irreductible
que estaba adentro, agazapado,
esperando con un espejo.
Es mucho mejor ir al cine
o conversar con las mujeres
o leer la historia de Egipto,
o estimular la complacencia,
la numismática o la iglesia.

Los que se dedican a Dios
de cuando en cuando, están salvados.
Llenos de ungüento medioeval
regresan a sus oficinas
o se dan un soplo de infierno
o usan dentífrico divino.

Los que no queremos a Dios
desde que Dios no quiere a nadie,
llegamos al campo, temprano,
a Rumay, junto a Melipilla,
y nos pensamos lentamente,
nos rechazamos con fervor,
con paciencia nos desunimos
y nos juntamos otra vez
para seguir siendo los mismos.

EL VIENTO

Pero no hay nada como el viento
de los duros montes, el agua

that person we used to be,
facing the essence
that lived inside us, caught,
waiting around with a mirror.
It is better to go to the movies
or converse with women
or read the history of Egypt,
or encourage complacency,
numismatics, or the church.

Those who devote themselves to God
from time to time, they are saved.
Covered with medieval ointment
they return to their offices
or take a gust of hell
or use divine toothpaste.

Those of us who do not love God
as God does not love anyone,
arrive in the countryside, early,
in Rumay, close to Melipilla,
and we reflect on ourselves,
we deny ourselves with fervor,
with patience we split apart
and come back together again
so to go on being ourselves.

THE WIND

But there is nothing like the wind
in the rugged mountains, the irrigation

de riego en los fríos canales,
el espacio inmóvil, la luz
colmando la copa del mundo
y el olor verde de la tierra.

Por eso tengo que volver
a tantos sitios venideros
para encontrarme conmigo
y examinarme sin cesar,
sin más testigo que la luna
y luego silbar de alegría
pisando piedras y terrones,
sin más tarea que existir,
sin más familia que el camino.

LA MÚSICA

Si no me enseñaron la tierra,
si sólo para recorrerla,
si nunca entré con el arado,
si no viví con los terrones
ni dormí sobre la cebada
no puedo hablar con los violines
porque la música es terrestre.

Pero es terrestre la cintura
de mi mejor enamorada
y tiene tierra el porvenir,
todas las cosas son de tierra.

water in the cold canals,
the motionless space, the light
filling to the brim the wineglass of the world,
and the green scent of the earth.

For that reason I have to go back
to so many places in the future
to find myself
and examine myself without rest,
with the moon my only witness
and then to whistle with happiness
stepping on stones and lumps of earth
with nothing to do other than exist,
with no family but the road.

THE MUSIC

If they did not show me the earth,
if only to travel over it,
if I never entered with the plow,
if I did not live with the clods of earth
nor sleep on the barley,
I could not speak with violins
because the music is of the earth.

But the waist of my greatest love
is of the earth,
and the future is earth,
all things are earth.

Es de tierra el pan, el silencio,
el fuego es el polvo que arde,
el agua es la tierra que corre
y todos los sueños nocturnos
vienen del fondo de la tierra.

METAMORFOSIS

He recibido un puntapié
del tiempo y se ha desordenado
el triste cajón de la vida.
El horario se atravesó
como doce perdices pardas
en un camino polvoriento
y lo que antes fue la una
pasó a ser las ocho cuarenta
y el mes de abril retrocedió
hasta transformarse en noviembre.

Los papeles se me perdieron,
no se encontraban los recibos,
se llenaron los basureros
con nombres de contribuyentes,
con direcciones de abogados
y números de deliciosas.

Fue una catástrofe callada.

Comenzó todo en un domingo
que en vez de sentirse dorado
se arrepintió de la alegría

Bread is earth, silence,
the fire is dust that burns,
water is the earth that flows,
and all dreams, night after night,
come from the depths of the earth.

METAMORPHOSIS

I have taken a kick
from time and it is now a mess,
the sad box of my life.
The timeline has stretched
like twelve brown partridges
across a dusty road,
and what before was one o'clock
came to be 8:40
and the month of April went backward
until turning into November.

My papers were lost,
receipts could not be found,
the garbage cans were filled
with names of contributors,
with addresses of lawyers
and numbers of beautiful women.

It was a quiet catastrophe.

Everything began on a Sunday,
which instead of feeling golden
repented its joy

y se portó tan lentamente
como una tortuga en la playa:
no llegó nunca al día lunes.

Al despertarme me encontré
más descabellado que nunca,
sin precedentes, olvidado
en una semana cualquiera,
como una valija en un tren
que rodara a ninguna parte
sin conductor ni pasajeros.

No era un sueño porque se oyó
un mugido espeso de vaca
y luego trajeron la leche
con calor aún de las ubres,
además de que me rodeaba
un espectáculo celeste:
la travesura de los pájaros
entre las hojas y la niebla.

Pero lo grave de este asunto
es que no continuaba el tiempo.
Todo seguía siendo sábado
hasta que el viernes se asomaba.

Adónde voy? Adónde vamos?
A quién podía consultar?

Los monumentos caminaban
hacia atrás, empujando el día
como guardias inexorables.

and bore itself as slowly
as a turtle on the beach:
it never arrived at Monday.

Waking up, I found myself
more disheveled than ever,
without precedent, forgotten
in a normal week,
like a suitcase on a train
that rolled nowhere,
with no conductor or passengers.

It was not a dream for it could be heard,
the thick mooing of a cow,
then they brought the milk
still warm from the udders,
and what surrounded me there
was a heavenly spectacle:
the mischief of birds
among the leaves and the fog.

But the gravity of this matter
is that time ceased moving.
All went on being Saturday
until Friday showed its face.

Where am I going? Where are we going?
With whom could we consult?

The monuments were striding
backward, shoving the day
like guards without pity.

Y se desplomaba hacia ayer
todo el horario del reloj.

No puedo mostrar a la gente
mi colección de escalofríos:
me sentí solo en una casa
perforada por las goteras
de un aguacero inapelable
y para no perder el tiempo,
que era lo único perdido,
rompí los últimos recuerdos,
me despedí de mi botica,
eché al fuego los talonarios,
las cartas de amor, los sombreros,
y como quien se tira al mar
yo me tiré contra el espejo.

Pero ya no me pude ver.
Sentía que se me perdía
el corazón precipitado
y mis brazos disminuyeron,
se desmoronó mi estatura,
a toda velocidad
se me borraban los años,
regresó mi cabellera,
mis dientes aparecieron.

En un fulgor pasé mi infancia,
seguí contra el tiempo en el cauce
hasta que no vi de mí mismo,
de mi retrato en el espejo
sino una cabeza de mosca,

And leaning toward yesterday
were all the hours of the clock.

I cannot show people
my collection of shivers:
I felt lonely in a house
riddled with leaks
in a downpour that heard no appeal,
and so as not to lose time,
which was the only thing lost,
I shattered my last memories,
I said goodbye to my medicine cabinet,
I threw my checkbook into the fire,
my love letters, hats,
and like he who leaps into the sea
I threw myself against the mirror.

I could no longer see myself.
I felt myself losing
my hastened heart
and my arms drooped,
my stature crumbled,
at full speed
my years were being erased,
my hair grew back,
my teeth appeared.

My childhood flared past,
I flowed against time in the riverbed
until I could no longer see myself,
my portrait in the mirror,
except as the head of a fly,

un microscópico huevillo,
volviendo otra vez al ovario.

EL ESTRELLERO

Me pongo a estrellar lo que falta
en el firmamento nocturno
con tan constante condición
que volando todos los días
vi mis pobres astros campestres
desencadenar la hermosura,
y estrellas que yo fabriqué
no parecían fabricadas:
todo parecía mejor
en el pavimento celeste.

Fue de pequeño que aprendí
a mirar las botellas rotas,
a esconder en la oscuridad
del subterráneo del Liceo
aquellos fragmentos de vidrio
en los que yo precipité
las vocaciones espaciales.

Acumulé clavos torcidos,
herraduras deshabitadas,
todo lo dispuse allí
clasificando con paciencia,
estimulando con astucia,
educando con energía,
hasta que pude despertar

a large microscopic egg
returning again to the ovary.

Maker of Stars

I set about filling with stars empty places
in the night sky
with such constancy
that flying day after day
I saw my poor rustic stars
unleash their beauty,
and stars I constructed
did not appear constructed:
everything looked better
in the steppingstones of the heavens.

When I was small I learned
to watch for broken bottles,
to conceal in the darkness
of the cellar of my Liceo
those shards of glass:
for them, I hastened
their calling as stars.

I collected bent nails,
empty horseshoes,
I laid out everything there
patiently classifying,
cleverly encouraging,
energetically educating,
until I was able to awaken

la fosforescencia del vidrio,
el frenesí de los metales.

Equiparado por la edad
a los sabios más eminentes
y hechicero como ninguno
logré asumir la posesión
del tesoro de mi subsuelo,
y premunido de herramientas
hereditarias, insondables,
construí primero una ráfaga
y luego un vuelo de luciérnagas.

El cometa me costó más.
Una estrella de cola ardiente,
una desposada del cielo,
una náufraga del espacio,
un elemento natural
lleno de velos y de luz
como un pez plateado de China
convocado en el coliseo
de Aldebarán y de Saturno
pareció difícil de hacer
hasta que de nieve y botellas
propulsado por su fulgor
subió de mis manos un astro
caudal, nupcial y vaporoso.

Luego de ilustres tentativas
desencadené un meteoro
elaborado con los restos
de mi subterráneo natal.
De tumbo en tumbo rodó

the phosphorescence of glass,
the frenzy of metals.

Compared at the time
to the most eminent sages
and a wizard like none other,
I managed to take possession
of the treasures of my substrata,
and equipped with hereditary
tools, unfathomable,
I first constructed a gust
and then a flight of fireflies.

The comet cost me more.
A star of burning tail,
newlywed of the sky,
shipwreck of space,
one natural element
full of veils and of light
like a silvery fish of China
summoned in the coliseum
of Aldebaran and of Saturn,
it looked hard to build
until from snow and bottles
propelled by its own radiance
it rose from my hands, a heavenly body
with a tail, nuptial and vaporous.

After illustrious attempts
I unleashed a meteor
made from the ruins
of the cellar of my birth.
From one jolt to the next, the meteor

en el espacio el meteoro
con todos los clavos secretos
de mi total ferretería.
Sonaron los astros quebrados
por el mandoble de mis dedos,
por mi estallido celeste,
y la noche se estremeció
recibiendo la catarata.

Así me entretuve, señores,
en el colegio de mi infancia.

El XIX

Lo curioso es que en este siglo
Mozart, el suave enlevitado,
continuó con su levitón,
con su vestido de música:
en estos cien años apenas
se escucharon otros ruidos,
y Fiódor Dostoyevski aún
desarrolla su folletín,
su dictamen de las tinieblas,
su larga cinta con espinas.

Bueno, y Rimbaud? Gracias, muy bien
contesta el vago vagabundo
que aún se pasea solitario
sin otra sombra en este siglo.

tumbled through space
with all the secret nails
of my entire metal shop.
The smashed stars rang out
with each swordlike blow of my fingers,
with my own celestial explosion,
and the night shuddered
welcoming the waterfall.

This is how, ladies and gentlemen,
I entertained myself
at the school of my childhood.

The XIX

It is curious, but in this century
Mozart, the graceful levitator,
still wore his heavy frock coat,
his suit of music:
during those hundred years, rarely
were other sounds heard,
and Fyodor Dostoyevsky still
rolls out his serial chapters,
his opinion of utter darkness,
his long ribbon with thorns.

All right, and Rimbaud? Thank you, very well,
replies the wandering wanderer
who still gets around by himself
with no other shadow in this century.

Yo que llegué desde Parral
a conocer este siglo,
por qué me dan el mismo frío,
el mismo plato, el mismo fuego
de los amables abuelitos
o de los abuelos amargos?

Hasta cuándo llueve Verlaine
sobre nosotros? Hasta cuándo
el paraguas de Baudelaire
nos acompaña a pleno sol?
Queremos saber dónde están
las araucarias que nacieron,
las encinas del Siglo Veinte,
dónde están las manos, los dedos,
los guantes de nuestra centuria.
Walt Whitman no nos pertenece,
se llama Siglo Diecinueve,
pero nos sigue acompañando
porque nadie nos acompaña.
Y en este desierto lanzó
el *sputnik* su polen rojo
entre las estrellas azules.

El siglo veinte se consume
con el siglo pasado a cuestas
y los pálidos escritores
bajo los gigantes muertos
hemos subido la escalera
con un saco sobre los hombros,
con la pesada precedencia
de los huesos más eminentes.

I who arrived from Parral
to know this century,
why am I offered the same cold,
the same plate, the same fire
of kindly grandparents
or of bitter grandparents?

How long will Verlaine rain
over us? Until when will
the umbrella of Baudelaire
accompany us in the sunlight?
We want to know where they are,
the araucarias that were born,
the oak trees of the twentieth century,
where, the hands, the fingers,
the gloves of our century.
Walt Whitman does not belong to us,
that century is called the nineteenth,
but he continues to accompany us
because no one accompanies us.
And across this desert Sputnik
scatters its red pollen
among the blue stars.

The twentieth century wastes away
with the past century borne on its shoulders,
and we writers, pale
beneath the dead giants,
have climbed the stairs
with a sack over our shoulders,
with the weighty precedent
of the most eminent bones.

Pesa Balzac un elefante,
Victor Hugo como un camión,
Tolstói como una cordillera,
como una vaca Émile Zola,
Emilia Brontë como un nardo,
Mallarmé como un pastelero,
y todos juntos aplastándonos
no nos dejaban respirar,
no nos dejaban escribir,
no nos querían dejar,
hasta que el tío Ubu Dada
los mandó a todos a la mierda.

Balzac weighs as much as an elephant,
Victor Hugo as much as a truck,
Tolstoy as much as a mountain range,
as much as a cow, Émile Zola,
Emily Brontë as much as spikenard,
Mallarmé as much as a pastry chef,
and all together, crushing us,
thwarting our breathing,
thwarting our writing,
they wouldn't leave us alone,
until Uncle Ubu Dada
sent them all to hell.

V

Como poeta carpintero
busco primero la madera
áspera o lisa, predispuesta:
con las manos toco el olor,
huelo el color, paso los dedos
por la integridad olorosa,
por el silencio del sistema,
hasta que me duermo o transmigro
o me desnudo y me sumerjo
en la salud de la madera,
en sus circunvalaciones.

Lo segundo que hago es cortar
con sierra de chisporroteo
la tabla recién elegida:
de la tabla salen los versos
como astillas emancipadas,
fragantes, fuertes y distantes
para que ahora mi poema
tenga piso, casco, carena,
se levante junto al camino,
sea habitado por el mar.

Como poeta panadero
preparo el fuego, la harina,
la levadura, el corazón,
y me complico hasta los codos,
amasando la luz del horno,

V

Ars Poetica (I)

As a poet-carpenter
I first seek the wood
rough or smooth, so inclined
with my hands I touch the scent,
I smell the color, pass my fingers
over the fragrant integrity,
through the silence of the system,
until I sleep or pass to another body,
or take off my clothes or submerge myself
in the health of the wood,
in its round ramparts.

The second thing I do is cut
with the sizzling saw
the table recently selected:
from the table rise the verses
like liberated splinters,
fragrant, strong and distant,
and so now, my poem,
have a deck, a hull, careening,
arise beside the road,
be inhabited by the sea.

As a poet-baker
I prepare the fire, the flour,
the leavening, the heart,
and I, involved up to the elbows,
kneading the light of the oven,

el agua verde del idioma,
para que el pan que me sucede
se venda en la panadería.

Yo soy y no sé si lo sepan
tal vez herrero por destino
o por lo menos propicié
para todos y para mí
metalúrgica poesía.

En tal abierto patrocinio
no tuve adhesiones ardientes:
fui ferretero solitario.

Rebuscando herraduras rotas
me trasladé con mis escombros
a otra región sin habitantes,
esclarecida por el viento.
Allí encontré nuevos metales
que fui convirtiendo en palabras.

Comprendo que mis experiencias
de metafísico manual
no sirvan a la poesía,
pero yo me dejé las uñas
arremetiendo a mis trabajos
y ésas son las pobres recetas
que aprendí con mis propias manos:
si se prueba que son inútiles
para ejercer la poesía
estoy de inmediato de acuerdo:
me sonrío para el futuro
y me retiro de antemano.

the green water of language,
so the bread that happens to me
sells itself in the bakery.

I am, and know not whether they know it,
a blacksmith by destiny
or at least I sponsored
for everyone and for myself
metallurgical poetry.

With such open patronage
I did not forge ardent bonds:
I was a solitary ironmonger.

Seeking broken horseshoes
I flowed with my slag
to a region without inhabitants,
illuminated by the wind.
There I found new metals
that I converted into words.

I understand that my experiences
as a metaphysician of hands
may not serve poetry,
but I grew out my claws
attacking my works,
and those are the poor recipes
I learned with my own hands:
if they are proved useless
in the practice of poetry,
I immediately relent:
I smile for the future
and retire in advance.

No he descubierto nada yo,
ya todo estaba descubierto
cuando pasé por este mundo.
Si regreso por estos lados
les pido a los descubridores
que me guarden alguna cosa,
un volcán que no tenga nombre,
un madrigal desconocido,
la raíz de un río secreto.

Fui siempre tan aventurero
que nunca tuve una aventura
y las cosas que descubrí
estaban dentro de mí mismo,
de tal modo que defraudé
a Juan, a Pedro y a María,
porque por más que me esforcé
no pude salir de mi casa.

Contemplé con envidia intensa
la inseminación incesante,
el ciclo de los sateloides,
la añadidura de esqueletos,
y en la pintura vi pasar
tantas maneras fascinantes
que apenas me puse a la moda
ya aquella moda no existía.

Ars Poetica (II)

I have not discovered anything,
everything was already discovered
by the time I passed through this world.
If I return to these parts
I shall ask the discoverers
to leave something for me,
a volcano with no name,
an unknown madrigal,
the root of a secret river.

I was always so adventurous
I never had an adventure,
and the things I did discover
were inside of me,
such that I let down
John, Peter, and Mary,
because no matter how hard I tried
I was not able to leave my house.

With intense envy I contemplated
the ceaseless sowing of seed,
the cycle of the satellites,
the added weight of skeletons,
and in painting I saw come and go
so many fascinating styles
I barely got up to speed
before that style had passed.

Abejas (I)

Qué voy a hacerle, yo nací
cuando habían muerto los dioses
y mi insufrible juventud
siguió buscando entre las grietas:
ése fue mi oficio y por eso
me sentí tan abandonado.

Una abeja más una abeja
no suman dos abejas claras
ni dos abejas oscuras:
suman un sistema de sol,
una habitación de topacio,
una caricia peligrosa.

La primera inquietud del ámbar
son dos abejas amarillas
y atado a las mismas abejas
trabaja el sol de cada día:
me da rabia enseñarles tanto
de mis ridículos secretos.

Me van a seguir preguntando
mis relaciones con los gatos,
cómo descubrí el arco iris,
por qué se vistieron de erizos
las beneméritas castañas,
y sobre todo que les diga
los que piensan de mí los sapos,
los animales escondidos
bajo la fragancia del bosque
o en las pústulas del cemento.

Bees (I)

What am I going to do, I was born
when the gods had already died,
and my insufferable youth
kept searching among the cracks:
it was my job, and for that reason
I felt so completely abandoned.

One bee and another bee
do not make two bright bees
or two dark bees:
they make a solar system,
a dwelling of topaz,
a dangerous caress.

Most worrisome for amber
are two yellow bees,
and tied to the same bees
the sun of each day labors:
it makes me furious to tell
so many of my silly secrets.

I keep getting asked
about my relationships with cats,
how I discovered the rainbow,
why the glorious chestnuts
dressed up as hedgehogs,
and, above all, that I tell
what the toads think of me,
the animals hidden
beneath the fragrance of the forest
or in pustules of cement.

Es la verdad que entre los sabios
he sido el único ignorante
y entre los que menos sabían
yo siempre supe un poco menos
y fue tan poco mi saber
que aprendí la sabiduría.

ABEJAS (II)

Hay un cementerio de abejas
allá en mi tierra, en Patagonia,
y vuelven con su miel a cuestas
a morir de tanta dulzura.

Es una región tempestuosa
curvada como una ballesta,
con un permanente arco iris
como una cola de faisán:
rugen los saltos de los ríos,
salta la espuma como liebre,
restalla el viento y se dilata
por la soledad circundante:
es un círculo la pradera
con la boca llena de nieve
y la barriga colorada.

Allí llegan una por una,
un millón junto a otro millón,
a morir todas las abejas

It is true that among the wise
I have been the only fool,
and among those who knew less
I always knew a little less,
and my knowing was so slight
that I learned wisdom.

BEES (II)

There is a cemetery of bees
there in my land, in Patagonia,
and they return with honey on their backs
to die of so much sweetness.

It is a stormy region
curved like a crossbow,
with a permanent rainbow,
like the tail of a pheasant:
the falls of the river roar,
the foam leaps like hare,
the wind cracks and expands
in the surrounding solitude:
the meadow is a circle,
its mouth full of snow
and its belly ruddy.

There they arrive one by one,
a million with another million,
all the bees arrive to die

hasta que la tierra se llena
de grandes montes amarillos.

No puedo olvidar su fragancia.

LA ROSA DEL HERBOLARIO

Dejo en la nave de la rosa
la decisión del herbolario:
si la estima por su virtud
o por la herida del aroma:
si es intacta como la quiere
o rígida como una muerta.

La breve nave no dirá
cuál es la muerte que prefiere:
si con la proa enarbolada
frente a su fuego victorioso
ardiendo con todas las velas
de la hermosura abrasadora
o secándose en un sistema
de pulcritud medicinal.

El herbolario soy, señores,
y me turban tales protestas
porque en mí mismo no convengo
a decidir mi idolatría:
la vestidura del rosal
quema el amor en su bandera
y el tiempo azota el esqueleto
derribando el aroma rojo

until the earth is covered
in great yellow mountains.

I will never forget their fragrance.

THE ROSE OF THE HERBALIST

I leave behind, on the ship of the rose,
the herbalist's determination:
whether he esteems it for its virtue
or for the wound of the aroma:
whether it is whole as he wants it
or as rigid as a dead one.

The fleeting ship will not say
which death it prefers:
whether with prow raised
facing its victorious fire,
flaring with all the sails
of the burning beauty,
or drying out in a regimen
of medicinal tidiness.

I, ladies and gentlemen, am the herbalist,
and such protests upset me,
for I do not arrange within myself
or decide what to idolize:
the clothes of the rosebush
burn love on its flag
and time whips the skeleton,
demolishing the red aroma

y la turgencia perfumada:
después con una sacudida
y una larga copa de lluvia
no queda nada de la flor.

Por eso agonizo y padezco
preservando el amor furioso
hasta en sus últimas cenizas.

AGUA

La desventaja del rocío
cuando su luz se multiplica
es que a la flor le nacen ojos
y estos ojos miran el mundo.

Ya dejaron de ser rocío.

Son las circunstancias del día:
reflexiones de la corola:
eternidad del agua eterna.

OTOÑO

Para la patria del topacio
designé una espiga infinita
y le agregué la ramazón
de la estirpe más amarilla:

son mis deberes en otoño.

and the scented turgidity:
later with a shaking
and a large glass of rain
nothing remains of the flower.

For that reason I agonize and suffer,
preserving the furious love
even in its final ashes.

WATER

The disadvantage of dew
when its light multiplies
is that to the flower eyes are born
and those eyes watch the world.

They are no longer dew.

They are circumstances of the day:
reflections of the corolla:
eternity of the eternal water.

AUTUMN

For the motherland of topaz
I designed an infinite spike of grain
and I gathered the pile of branches
of that most yellow lineage:

these, my autumnal duties.

ALIANZA

Cuando la hoja no converse
con otras hojas y preserve
infinitos labios el árbol
para susurrarnos susurros,
cuando la patria vegetal
con sus banderas abolidas
se resigne al precario idioma
del hombre o a su silencio
y por mi parte cuando asuma
como agua o savia los deberes
de la raíz a la corola,
ay ese mundo es la victoria,
es el paraíso perdido,
la unidad verde, la hermosura
de las uvas y de las manos,
el signo redondo que corre
anunciando mi nacimiento.

RAZÓN

La oblonga razón de la rama
parece inmóvil pero escucha
cómo suena la luz del cielo
en la cítara de sus hojas
y si te inclinas a saber
cómo sube el agua a la flor
oirás la luna cantar
en la noche de las raíces.

ALLIANCE

When the leaf does not converse
with other leaves, and the tree
preserves infinite lips
whispering us its whispers,
when the vegetal motherland
with its abolished flags
resigns itself to the precarious language
of man or to his silence,
and, for my part, when it assumes
like water or sap the duties
of the root to the corolla,
oh that world is the triumph,
it is the lost paradise,
the green unity, the beauty
of the grapes and of the hands,
the round sign that hurries
announcing my birth.

REASON

The oblong reason for the branch
appears motionless but listen
to how the sky's light sounds
in the zither of its leaves,
and if you are inclined to learn
how water climbs to the flower
you will hear the moon sing
in the night of the roots.

ÁRBOL

Anoche al apagar la luz
se me durmieron las raíces
y se me quedaron los ojos
enredados entre las hojas
hasta que, tarde, con la sombra
se me cayó una rama al sueño
y por el tronco me subió
la fría noche de cristal
como una iguana transparente.

Entonces me quedé dormido.

Cerré los ojos y las hojas.

SILENCIO

Yo que crecí dentro de un árbol
tendría mucho que decir,
pero aprendí tanto silencio
que tengo mucho que callar
y eso se conoce creciendo
sin otro goce que crecer,
sin más pasión que la substancia,
sin más acción que la inocencia,
y por dentro el tiempo dorado
hasta que la altura lo llama
para convertirlo en naranja.

TREE

Last night, when I put out the light
my roots fell asleep
and my eyes wound up
entangled among the leaves
until, late, with its shadow
a branch fell into my dream
and from the trunk climbed toward me
the cold crystalline night
like a transparent iguana.

Then I fell asleep.

I closed my eyes and my leaves.

SILENCE

I who grew inside a tree
should have much to say,
but I learned silence so well
I have a lot to keep quiet
that is aware it is growing
with no other pleasure than growing,
with no passion but substance,
with no action but innocence,
until within golden time
the heights call it
so as to convert it into oranges.

Unidad

Esta hoja son todas las hojas,
esta flor son todos los pétalos
y una mentira la abundancia.
Porque todo fruto es el mismo,
los árboles son uno solo
y es una sola flor la tierra.

La rosa

De una rosa a otra rosa había
tantos rosales de distancia
que me fui de una vida a otra
sin decidirme al arrebato
y cuando era tarde sin duda
muerto de amor me despedí
de toda mi triste entereza.
Volví a buscar aquel aroma,
la rosa roja del dolor
o la amarilla del olvido
o la blanca de la tristeza
o la insólita rosa azul:
lo cierto es que es vano volver
al país de la primavera:
era tan tarde que caían
las estrellas en el camino
y me detuve a recoger
el fulgor del trigo nocturno.

UNITY

All leaves are this leaf,
all petals are this flower,
and abundance a lie.
For all fruit is the same,
the trees are one, alone,
and the earth, a single flower.

THE ROSE

From one rose to the next I had
so many rosebushes of distance
that I went from one life to the next
not making up my mind about my rage,
and when it was undeniably late,
deadly in love I said goodbye
to every bit of my sad integrity.
I returned seeking that scent,
the red rose of pain
or the yellow of forgetting
or the white of sadness
or the uncommon blue rose:
certainly, we return only in vain
to the country of springtime:
I was so late that the stars
fell onto the road,
and I stopped to harvest
the splendor of the nocturnal wheat.

El malherido

Dejé las espinas caer
para no herir a nadie nunca,
por eso he llegado a esta página
entre desnudo y malherido.
Dejé caer las amarguras
para que no sufriera nadie
y tanto me hicieron sufrir
que me moriré de indefenso.

Cae la flor

Los siete pétalos del mar
se juntan en esta corola
con la diadema del amor:
sucedió todo en el vaivén
de una rosa que cayó al agua
cuando el río llegaba al mar.
Así un borbotón escarlata
saltó del día enamorado
a los mil labios de la ola
y una rosa se deslizó
hacia el sol y sobre la sal.

Bestiario (I)

El antílope clandestino
se desarrolla en la fogata:
su hocico se nutre de fuego
y su cola parece de humo.

The Wounded

I let fall the thorns
so no one would ever again be hurt,
and that is why I, naked and wounded,
have arrived at this page.
I let fall the bitternesses
so that no one would suffer,
and they made me suffer so much
I will die from having no defense.

The Flower Falls

The seven petals of the sea
united in this corolla
with the diadem of love:
everything swayed back and forth
with a rose that fell to the water
as the river was arriving at the sea.
In that way, a scarlet gushing
leapt from the loving day
to the thousand lips of the wave,
and a rose slipped
toward the sun and over the salt.

Bestiary (I)

The secret antelope
evolves in the bonfire:
its snout feeds on the flame
and its tail appears as smoke.

Van y vienen las llamaradas
por la corona cornamenta
y el animal, fiel a su signo,
resuelve el extraño sistema
de los ardientes alimentos
dejando como puntuaciones
detrás de su cola quemada
un collar tácito de ámbar.

BESTIARIO (II)

Inventando el ornitorrinco
me pasé los meses dorados
de aquel reino sin esperanza:
todos los días eran jueves
y se unía el mar con el aire
en una sola monarquía.

Repetí en aquel animal
los encarnizados plumajes
del cóndor amargo y patriota.
Me costó establecer el pico
del selvático personaje
y para sus patas, qué hacer?
Cómo dotarlo de naufragios,
de paroxismo, de señales?

Abrí mi cajón de esperpento
que acarreaba por esos mares

The flarings rise and fall
through the crown of horns,
and the animal, loyal to its crest,
overcomes the strange system
of smoldering sustenance,
leaving like punctuation
behind its flaming tail
an unsung collar of amber.

BESTIARY (II)

Inventing the platypus,
I spent the golden months
of that kingdom with no hope:
every day was Thursday
and the sea united with the air
in a single monarchy.

I repeated in that animal
the bloody feathers
of the bitter and patriotic condor.
It was hard to shape the bill
of this woodland character—
and for its legs, what to do?
How to endow them with shipwrecks,
with spasms, with signals?

I opened my box of fright
that I carried on those seas,

y sacando un huevo exquisito,
rectangular y tricolor,
soplé con loco frenesí,
con invención desesperada,
hasta que nació el desvarío
que se pasea por la selva.

ANIMAL

Aquel certero escarabajo
voló con élitros abiertos
hasta la cereza infrarroja.

La devoró sin comprender
la química del poderío
y luego volvió a los follajes
convertido en un incendiario.

Su caparazón derivó
como un cometa saturado
por la radiación deliciosa
y se fue ardiendo en la substancia
de tan quemantes electrones:

al disolverse alcanzó a ser
un síntoma del arco iris.

and taking out an exquisite egg,
rectangular and tricolored,
I blew with frenzied madness,
with desperate invention,
until it was born, the delirium
that walks the forest.

ANIMAL

That skillful beetle
flew with open elytra
to meet the infrared cherry.

It devoured it without comprehending
the chemistry of its power,
and soon it returned to the leaves
transformed into an incendiary.

Its shell canted
like a comet saturated
with delicious radiation,
and it flew flaming in the essence
of burning hot electrons:

dissolving, it became
a symptom of the rainbow.

PERRO

Los perros desinteresados
por los caminos, sin regreso,
por el polvo errante, a la luz
de la intemperie indiferente.

Oh Dios de los perros perdidos,
pequeño dios de patas tristes,
acércate a nuestro hemisferio
de largas colas humilladas,
de ojos hambrientos que persiguen
a la luna color de hueso!

Oh Dios descuidado, yo soy
poeta de las carreteras
y vago en vano sin hallar
un idioma de perrería
que los acompañe cantando
por la lluvia o la polvareda.

CABALLO

Me he preguntado muchas veces
al amanecer, cuando subo
a un esqueleto de caballo,
por qué el corcel no se desarma
entre los peñascos que cruzo
o las arboledas que paso
o las olas que dejo atrás

DOG

The disinterested dogs
along the roads, without returning,
through the wandering dust, to the light
of the indifferent wind and rain.

O God of lost dogs,
small god of sad legs,
come nearer to our hemisphere
of long humiliated tails,
of hungry eyes that chase
the bone-colored moon!

O careless God, I am
poet of the highways,
and I wander in vain, never finding
a language of the pack
which might accompany them singing
through the rain or the clouds of dust.

HORSE

I have asked myself many times
in the dawn, as I climb
onto a skeleton of a horse,
why the steed does not fall apart,
what with the crags I cross over
or the thickets I pass through
or the waves I leave behind

o la polvareda que sigue
mi insobornable cabalgata.

Oh caballo grabado en blanco
sobre el pizarrón estepario
de la patagónica noche,
cuando regreso galopando
en mi montura de ceniza
como inspector de torbellinos
o como coronel glacial
de los ventisqueros que ruedan
al mar con sus caballerías!

Después recojo las distancias,
vuelvo a mi sueño cotidiano,
apaciguo mis fundamentos
hasta que en el alba del frío
siento golpear las herraduras
y me despierto a recorrer
el invierno recién llegado
con mi caballo transparente.

OTRO PERRO

Perseguí por aquellas calles
a un perro errante, innecesario,
para saber adónde van
de noche trotando los perros.

Sólo mil veces se detuvo
a orinar en sitios remotos

or the dust cloud that follows
my incorruptible ride.

Oh horse engraved in white
on the blackboard steppe
of the Patagonian night,
as I return galloping
on my mount of ash,
an inspector of whirling winds,
or as a glacial colonel
of glaciers rolling onward
to the sea with their cavalry.

After I gather the distances,
I return to my everyday dream,
I soothe my essence
until in the dawning of the cold
I feel the beating of horseshoes,
and I awake to ride through
the recently arrived winter
on my transparent horse.

ANOTHER DOG

Through those streets I chased
a wandering dog, unwanted,
to find out where they go
at night, the trotting dogs.

Only a thousand times he stopped
to pee in remote places

y siguió como si tuviera
que recibir un telegrama.

Pasó casas y cruzó esquinas,
parques, aldeas y países,
y yo detrás del caminante
para saber adónde iba.

Siguió sin fin sobrepasando
los barrios llenos de basura,
los puentes desiertos e inútiles
cuando dormían los carruajes.

Los regimientos, las escuelas,
las estatuas de bronce muerto,
la tristeza de los prostíbulos
y los cabarets fatigados,
cruzamos, el perro adelante
y yo, cansado como un perro.

PEZ

Aquel pez negro de Acapulco
me miró con ojos redondos
y regresó a la transparencia
de su océano de anilina:
vi sus bigotes despedir
unas cuantas gotas de mar
que resplandecieron, celestes.

and went on as though he were
picking up a telegram.

He passed houses and crossed corners,
parks, villages, and countries,
and I stayed behind that drifter
to see where he was going.

He ceaselessly passed beyond
the quarters full of rubbish,
the deserted and useless bridges
when the carriages were sleeping.

The regiments, the schools,
the statues of dead bronze,
the sadness of the brothels
and the weary cabarets,
we cross, the dog trotting ahead
and I, tired as a dog.

FISH

That black fish from Acapulco
watched me with round eyes
and returned to the clarity
of its ocean of aniline:
I saw its whiskers give off
several drops of sea
that shined, like the stars.

Y cuando cayó de mi anzuelo
volviendo al susurro entreabierto
de la piedra y del agua azul
no había en sus ojos estáticos
reconocimiento ninguno
hacia la tierra, ni hacia el hombre.

Yo me sacudí de reír
por mi fracaso y por su cara
y él se deslizó a revivir
sin emociones, en el agua.

LA TIERRA

El lagartijo iridiscente,
la concha con alas de nácar,
las hojas de pangue excesivas
como las manos de Goliat,
y estos insectos que me siguen
me cantan y me continúan.

Oh cuántos relojes perversos
inventó la naturaleza
para que solidarizara
cada minuto de mi vida
y me lo pasara firmando
mi adhesión a sus invenciones:
a los cisnes, a las arañas,
a pájaros y mariposas.

And when it fell from my hook,
returning to the half-open whisper
of the stone and of the blue water,
it did not have in its static eyes
any recognition whatsoever
of the earth, nor of man.

I shook with laughter
at my failure and in his face,
and he slipped back into life
with no emotion, in the water.

THE EARTH

The small iridescent lizard,
the shell with wings of mother-of-pearl,
the leaves of giant rhubarb
like the hands of Goliath,
and these insects follow me
singing to me, a part of me.

Oh, how many perverse clocks
nature invented
so that each minute of my life
be solidified
and that I spend my time pledging
my allegiance to its inventions:
to the swans, to the spiders,
to birds and butterflies.

De tanto fulgor refulgí
como los colores del agua
y tuve olor a barro negro
donde se pudren las raíces:
tuve voz de rana sombría,
dedos de puma adolescente,
mirada triste de abejorro,
pies de pésimo paquidermo,
testículos de callampa,
ombligo serio como el ojo
de un antiguo caballo tuerto,
piernas de perro perseguido
y corazón de escarabajo.

BODAS

De qué sirve un ciervo sin cierva,
de qué sirve un perro sin perra,
una abeja sin su abejo,
una tigresa sin su tigre,
o una camella sin camello,
o una ballena sin balleno
o un rinoceronte soltero?

De qué sirve un gato sin gata,
un ruiseñor sin ruiseñora,
una paloma sin palomo,
un caballito sin caballa,
una cangreja sin cangrejo,
un agujero sin raíces?

With such brilliance I blazed
like the colors of water,
and smelled of black mud
where the roots rot:
my voice was a somber frog's,
fingers of an adolescent puma,
sad look of a bumblebee,
feet of abominable pachyderm,
testicles of fungus,
navel serious as the eye
of a one-eyed antique horse,
legs of chased dog
and heart of beetle.

WEDDINGS

What use is a stag without a doe,
what use is a dog without bitch,
a bee without her worker bee,
a tigress without her tiger,
or a he-camel without she-camel,
or a whale without male whale,
or a single rhinoceros?

What use is a cat without she-cat,
nightingale without a night in gala,
a dove without a manly dove,
a jackal without a mackerel,
a spanker with no sea crab,
a hole with no roots.

A casarse, peces del mar,
pumas de la pumería,
zorros de cola engañosa,
pulgas hambrientas de provincia.

A procrear! dice la tierra
con una voz tan invisible
que todos la ven y la tocan
y todos la oyen, y esperan.

Marry, fish of the sea,
pumas of the cougarland,
foxes of illusive tail,
hungry country fleas.

Give birth! says the earth
with a voice so invisible
that everyone sees and feels it,
everyone hears it, and they hope.

VI

Todos los poetas excelsos
se reían de mi escritura
a causa de la puntuación,
mientras yo me golpeaba el pecho
confesando puntos y comas,
exclamaciones y dos puntos,
es decir, incestos y crímenes
que sepultaban mis palabras
en una Edad Media especial
de catedrales provincianas.

Todos los que nerudearon
comenzaron a vallejarse
y antes del gallo que cantó
se fueron con Perse y con Eliot
y murieron en su piscina.
Mientras tanto yo me enredaba
con mi calendario ancestral
más anticuado cada día
sin descubrir sino una flor
descubierta por todo el mundo,
sin inventar sino una estrella
seguramente ya apagada,
mientras yo embebido en su brillo,
borracho de sombra y de fósforo,
seguía el cielo estupefacto.

VI

All the lofty poets
chuckled at my writing
on account of my punctuation,
while I beat my chest
confessing periods and commas,
exclamation points and colons,
which is to say, incests and crimes
that buried my words
in a special Middle Ages
and its provincial cathedrals.

Everyone who played neruda
began by playing vallejo
and before the rooster that sang
they left with Perse and with Eliot
and died in their pool.
Meanwhile I became tangled up
in my ancestral calendar
more obsolete each day,
discovering only a flower
discovered by the whole world,
inventing only a star
surely, by now, burned out,
while I drank in its splendor,
drunk on shadow and matchstick,
pursuing the astonished sky.

La próxima vez que regrese
con mi caballo por el tiempo
voy a disponerme a cazar
debidamente agazapado
todo lo que corra o que vuele:
a inspeccionarlo previamente
si está inventado o no inventado,
descubierto o no descubierto:
no se escapará de mi red
ningún planeta venidero.

SE LLENÓ EL MUNDO

Hermosos fueron los objetos
que acumuló el hombre tardío,
el voraz manufacturante:
conocí un planeta desnudo
que poco a poco se llenó
con los lingotes triturados,
con los limones de aluminio,
con los intestinos eléctricos
que sacudían a las máquinas
mientras el Niágara sintético
caía sobre las cocinas.

Ya no se podía pasar
en mil novecientos setenta
por las calles y por los campos:
las locomotoras raídas,
las penosas motocicletas,
los fracasados automóviles,

The next time I return
with my horse through time
I am going to prepare myself to hunt
properly, bagging
everything that runs or flies:
to inspect it beforehand
to see whether it has or has not been invented,
discovered or not discovered:
it will not escape my net,
not any planet to come.

THE WORLD FILLED UP

Beautiful were the objects
the late man accumulated,
the voracious manufacturer:
I knew a naked planet
that little by little filled
with crushed ingots,
with aluminum lemons,
with electric intestines
that shook the machines
while synthetic Niagara
cascaded in the kitchens.

No one was able to pass
in nineteen seventy
through the streets or beyond the fields:
the threadbare locomotives,
the distressed motorcycles,
the failed automobiles,

las barrigas de los aviones
invadieron el fin del mundo:
no nos dejaban transitar
no nos dejaban florecer,
llenaban arenas y valles,
sofocaban los campanarios:

no se podía ver la luna.

Venecia desapareció
debajo de la gasolina,
Moscú creció de tal manera
que murieron los abedules
desde el Kremlin a los Urales
y Chicago llegó tan alto
que se desplomó de improviso
como un cubilete de dados.

Vi volar el último pájaro
cerca de Mendoza, en los Andes.
Y recordándolo derramo
lágrimas de penicilina.

BOMBA (I)

Pero en estos años nació
la usina total de la muerte,
el núcleo desencadenado,
y no nos bastó asesinar
a cien mil japoneses dormidos,
sino que se perfeccionó

the bellies of the planes
invaded the end of the world:
they did not allow us to travel,
they did not allow us to flower,
they filled the sands and the valleys,
they suffocated the bell towers:

no one could see the moon.

Venice disappeared
beneath gasoline,
Moscow grew such
that the birches died
from the Kremlin to the Urals,
and Chicago grew so tall
it suddenly toppled over
like a cup of dice.

I saw the last bird fly
near Mendoza, in the Andes.
And remembering it, I shed
tears of penicillin.

BOMB (I)

But in these years was born
the whole factory of death,
the unchained nucleus,
and it was not enough for us to murder
one hundred thousand sleeping Japanese—
the tool, creator of sawdust,

la herramienta del aserrín
hasta alimentarla y pulirla,
fortificarla, fecundarla,
dejándola arriba colgando
sobre la cabeza del mundo.

Esperando están los neutrones
las ondas de ataque, los largos
dedos de la cohetería,
el asesinato orbital,
y así como la tierra pura
nos prepara la primavera,
así con cuidado exquisito
entre guantes y gabinetes
hay otra fiesta preparada:
el suicidio del universo.

Yo conozco el humo del bosque
y toqué la ceniza verde
de las montañas olorosas
y luego viví bajo el humo
de la ciudad recalcitrante
y de sus panaderías.

Pero más tarde conocí
en España de mis dolores
el humo del la destrucción,
y odio hasta ahora ese recuerdo
porque no hay humo más amargo
que el humo inútil de la guerra.

Y ahora un planeta de humo
nos espera a todos los hombres:

was brought to perfection,
feeding it and polishing it,
fortifying it, making it fertile,
hanging it high
over the head of the world.

The neutrons are awaiting
the waves of attack, the long
fingers of the missile silos,
the orbiting assassination,
and just as the pure earth
prepares spring for us,
with such exquisite care
among gloves and laboratories
is prepared another festivity:
the suicide of the universe.

I know the smoke of the forest
and touched the green ash
of the sweet-smelling mountains,
and later I lived beneath the smoke
of the defiant city
and its bakeries.

But later I came to know
in the Spain of my sorrows
the smoke of annihilation,
and even now I hate that memory
because no smoke is more bitter
than the needless smoke of war.

And now a planet of smoke
awaits all men:

no nos podremos saludar,
los muertos bajo los escombros,
se terminarán las palabras,
los idiomas serán quemados
y pondrá veneno en las flores
la primavera radioactiva
para que caigan en pedazos
el fruto muerto, el pan podrido.

Así somos

Si ustedes saben cómo se hace
díganmelo y no me lo digan:
porque aunque tarde he comprendido
que no lo sé, ni lo sabré,
y de tanto no haber sabido
sobreviviendo a mi ignorancia
creyeron que yo lo sabía.

Yo los creía mentirosos:
pero después del sufrimiento
su mentira fue mi verdad.

(Cómo se hace para saber?
Para no saber cómo se hace?
Y los sabios de la mentira
siguen diciendo la verdad?)

we will not be able to greet each other,
dead and buried under the debris,
words will come to an end,
all language will be burned
and the radioactive spring
will infuse flowers with poison
sending these to pieces,
the dead fruit, the rotten bread.

As We Are

If you know how it is done
tell me and do not tell me:
because, though I came to understand late
that I do not know nor ever will know,
and, for all that unknowing
outlasting my ignorance,
you believed I knew.

I thought them liars:
but after the suffering
their lie became my truth.

(How is it done, this not knowing?
So as to not know how it is done?
And do the sages of deceit
go on telling the truth?)

Dicen que ha muerto Neponiavsky
dentro de un tanque y hacia Praga
con su máquina de escribir
en la maldita coyuntura.
No sé si por melancolía
me deja duro la noticia.
Conocí sus ojos brillantes,
su periodismo intransigente:
fuimos amigos, sin embargo,
no quería que lo quisieran:
era un héroe de nuestro tiempo:
fue devorado por un tanque.

Preparémonos a morir
en mandíbulas maquinarias,
preparemos piernas, espaldas,
meditaciones y caderas,
codos, rodillas, entusiasmo,
párpados y sabiduría
serán tragados, triturados
y digeridos por un tanque.

Debo cumplir con mi deber:
hacerme aceitoso y sabroso
para que me coma una máquina
en una calle o una plaza
y arroje luego a la basura
las durezas de mi esqueleto.

Hay que buscarles carne tierna
de niños bien amamantados

DEATH OF A JOURNALIST

They say Neponiavsky has died
inside a tank and near Prague
with his typewriter
in that cursed circumstance.
I do not know whether out of melancholy
the news hardened my heart.
I knew his brilliant eyes,
his resolute journalism:
and though we were friends
I did not want him to be loved:
he was a hero of our time:
he was devoured by a tank.

Let us prepare ourselves to die
in the jaws of machinery,
let us prepare legs, backs,
meditations and hips,
elbows, knees, enthusiasm,
eyelids and wisdom,
they will be swallowed up, ground up,
and digested by a tank.

I must do my duty:
make myself oily and tasty
so a machine consumes me
in a street or a plaza
and after throws in the garbage
the tougher parts of my skeleton.

We need to seek out the tender meat
of well-breast-fed children

para que cuando trepidando
se desate la maquinaria
y abran la boca sus cañones
implorándonos alimentos,
comprendamos nuestro deber:
hay que morir para saciarlos.

Es nuestra época pesada,
la edad de las patas de fierro,
el siglo sangriento y redondo,
y debemos reconocer
las ruedas del Apocalipsis.

Los motores enmascarados
desempeñaron sus trayectos
dirigidos por la agonía
y necesitan devorar:
parece pues innecesario
negarse a los devoradores
y hay que proclamar con ardor
que queremos ser devorados.

Después de todo no sirvieron
las frágiles torres humanas,
todo fue blando o quebradizo,
toda pintura se perfora,
no nos defiende una sonata,
los libros arden y se van.

El siglo negro se prepara
para morir con elegancia
en el otoño del mundo:
no le daremos este gusto:

so that when the machinery,
shuddering, begins to rage,
and its cannons open their mouths
begging us for nourishment,
we embrace our duty:
to satisfy them, we must die.

It is our heavy epoch,
the age of iron paws,
the bloody and circular century,
and we must recognize
the wheels of the Apocalypse.

The masked engines
set out upon their routes
guided by agony,
and they need to eat:
thus it seems useless
to refuse those who devour,
and we must passionately proclaim
that we want devouring.

After all, they did not serve us,
the fragile human towers,
everything was soft and breakable,
any painting may be riddled with holes,
a sonata does not defend us,
the books burn and pass on.

The black century prepares itself
to die with style
in the autumn of the world:
let us not give it this pleasure:

vamos a escupirle la cara
y a echarlo debajo de un tanque.

RESURRECCIONES

Si alguna vez vivo otra vez
será de la misma manera
porque se puede repetir
mi nacimiento equivocado
y salir con otra corteza
cantando la misma tonada.

Y por eso, por si sucede,
si por un destino indostánico
me veo obligado a nacer,
no quiero ser un elefante,
ni un camello desvencijado,
sino un modesto langostino,
una gota roja del mar.

Quiero hacer en el agua amarga
las mismas equivocaciones:
ser sacudido por la ola
como ya lo fui por el tiempo
y ser devorado por fin
por dentaduras del abismo,
así como fue mi experiencia
de negros dientes literarios.

Pasear con antenas de cobre
en las antárticas arenas

let's spit in its face
and throw it beneath a tank.

RESURRECTIONS

If ever I live again
it will be in the same way
because my mistaken birth
is able to repeat itself,
to leave wearing other rough bark
and singing the same tune.

And for that reason, if it happens that way,
if by some Hindustani destiny
I find myself bound to be born,
I do not want to be an elephant
or some ramshackle camel,
more like a humble prawn,
a red drop of the sea.

I want to make in bitter water
the same mistakes:
to be shaken by the wave
as I once was by time,
and to be finally devoured
by teeth of the abyss,
like my experiences
of literary black teeth.

To take a walk with copper antennae
along the Antarctic sands

del litoral que amé y viví,
deslizar un escalofrío
entre las algas asustadas,
sobrevivir bajo los peces
escondiendo el caparazón
de mi complicada estructura,
así es como sobreviví
a las tristezas de la tierra.

SIGLO

Con apenas alas y ruedas
nació el año número uno
del mil novecientos año
y ahora que se va enterrando
si bien tiene piernas podridas,
ojos sangrientos, uñas tristes,
tiene más ruedas que jamás,
tiene alas para todo el cielo.

Vamos volando, nos invita
con el corazón a cuestas
arrastrando por el espacio
un saco impúdico de crímenes:
lo vemos subir y subir
agujereando la estratósfera
y dejando atrás el sonido.
No sólo nosotros oímos
el cuchillo que clava el cielo
y que recorta los planetas:
en islas malditas lo siguen

of the coast that I loved and lived,
a shiver slipping
amid the frightened seaweed,
to survive beneath the fish
concealing the shell
of my complicated structure,
that is how I survived
the sadnesses of the earth.

CENTURY

Scarcely with wings or wheels
was born the first year
of the nineteen hundreds
and now that it passes, burying,
even with its rotten legs,
bloody eyes, sad fingernails,
it has more wheels than ever,
it has wings for the entire sky.

We go flying, and it invites us
with its heart on its back,
carrying through space
a shameless sack of crimes:
we see it climb and climb
poking holes in the stratosphere
and leaving behind the sound.
It is not only we who hear
the knife that stabs the sky
and trims the planets:
on cursed islands they track it,

los poetas encadenados
de Atenas, y en los calabozos
de las prisiones paraguayas
celebran el fruto espacial
los ojos de los torturados.

Tal vez pensamos que la dicha
nos ofrecerá sus planetas
y que debemos alejar
la mirada de la agonía.
No nos hagamos ilusiones
nos aconseja el calendario,
todo seguirá como sigue,
la tierra no tiene remedio:
en otras regiones celestes
hay que buscar alojamiento.

LA GUERRILLERA

Hace un año que en Astrolabia
murió una niña guerrillera,
bella como una cineraria.
Fue asesinada por los malos.
Con dolor y con alegría
los buenos mataron a un juez.
Los malos mataron entonces
a un estudiante valeroso.
Y anoche oímos que los buenos,
cumpliendo sus obligaciones,
mataron un veterinario.

the shackled poets
of Athens, and in cells
of Paraguayan prisons
they honor the fruit of space,
the eyes of the tortured.

Perhaps we think that happiness
will offer us its planets
and that we must turn
our gaze away from agony.
Let us not harbor illusions,
the calendar counsels us,
everything will go as it goes,
the earth is hopeless:
we must seek accommodations
in other starry regions.

THE CHILD GUERRILLA

It has been one year since in Astrolabia
a child guerrilla died,
beautiful as a cineraria.
She was murdered by bad men.
With sadness and with joy
the good men killed a judge.
The bad then murdered
a courageous student.
And tonight we hear that the good,
in fulfilling their duties,
killed a veterinarian.

Astrolabia es una angostura
de agua y volcán, es un recinto
de antigüedad y frutería:
allí se apretó la belleza
como un saquito de esmeralda.
Pero está muriendo Astrolabia
entre los buenos asesinos
y los asesinos malvados,
hasta que la dejen difunta
entre dos ametralladoras.

QUÉ PASÓ?

Se ha cargado el aire de letras:
floreció el secreto sonido:
se acercaron los continentes
y ya podemos adquirir
en el almacén venidero
pulmón recién reconstruido,
corazón de segunda mano.
Hay signos terrestres plantados
en las arenas de la luna:

son victorias, son amenazas?

son amarguras o dulzuras?

Para quedarnos satisfechos
las celebraremos llorando
o dispongámonos mejor
a llorarlas con alegría.

Astrolabia is a narrow stretch
of water and volcano, a precinct
of antiquity and fruitfulness:
the beauty squeezed itself
as into a small emerald sack.
But Astrolabia keeps on dying
between the good murderers
and the bad murderers—
till they leave her for dead
between two machine guns.

WHAT HAPPENED?

The air has become charged with letters:
the secret sound blossomed:
the continents drew together
and now we can purchase
from the warehouse of the future
a newly reconstructed lung,
a secondhand heart.
Earthly signs are planted
in the sands of the moon:

are they victories, are they threats?

are they resentments or delights?

To satisfy ourselves
we will celebrate them, weeping,
or better prepare ourselves
to weep for them with joy.

Un millón de horribles retratos
de Stalin cubrieron la nieve
con sus bigotes de jaguar.

Cuando supimos y sangramos
descubriendo tristeza y muerte
bajo la nieve en la pradera
descansamos de su retrato
y respiramos sin sus ojos
que amamantaron tanto miedo.

Cambió el color de la blancura:
floreció de nuevo la hierba.

Yo fui férreo en este dolor
y registrando los tormentos
dentro de mi alma desollada
después de cargar con la muerte
me puse a cargar con la duda
y luego es mejor el olvido
para sostener la esperanza.

Ignoraba lo que ignoramos.
Y aquella locura tan larga
estuvo ciega y enterrada
en su grandeza demencial
envuelta a veces por la guerra
o propalada en el rencor
por nuestros viejos enemigos.

The Worship (II)

A million horrible portraits
of Stalin covered the snow
with jaguar mustaches.

When we learned and bled—
discovering sorrow and death
beneath the snow in the meadow,
we broke from his portrait
and breathed without his eyes
that nursed so much fear.

The shade of whiteness changed:
the grass flourished anew.

I was like iron against this pain,
and registering the torments
inside my skinned soul
after the burden of death,
there came the burden of doubt,
and later it is better to forget
so as to sustain hope.

I was unaware of that which we were unaware.
And that madness, so long lasting,
was blind and buried
in its demented grandeur,
wrapped at times in the war
or spread in rancor
by our old enemies.

Sólo el espanto era invisible.

Fue la proliferación
de aquel impasible retrato
la que incubó lo desmedido.

Celebramos la frente dura
sin comprender que nos medía
bajo las cejas georgianas
la catadura del monarca,
la geología del terror.

Pero la luz se descubrió
y recobramos la razón:
no por un hombre y por su crimen
arrojaríamos el bien
a la bodega del malvado:
recuperamos el amor
y seguimos de pueblo en pueblo
mostrando al hombre la verdad
y la bandera venidera.

NUNCA MÁS

Ya no podían volver más
los retratos ni los monarcas,
ya no podría florecer
la primavera autoritaria:
la lección la enseñó la muerte
y levantamos la cabeza.

Only the fear was invisible.

It was the proliferation
of that steely portrait
that incubated the excesses.

We celebrate the hard brow,
not seeing it was sizing us up—
beneath those Georgian eyebrows,
the testing eyes of the monarch,
the geology of terror.

But light was discovered,
and we recovered our reason:
not for any man or his crime
would we throw the good
into the cellar of the wicked:
we resuscitated our love,
as we kept on from town to town
spreading among men the truth
and the future flag.

NEVER MORE

They could never again return,
the portraits or the monarchs,
no longer would the authoritarian spring
be able to flower:
death taught the lesson
and we raise our heads.

Así es de clara la verdad
aunque venga de noche oscura.

El culto (III)

Pero, silencio, que otra vez,
otra vez aparece un rostro
sin sonrisa ya para siempre
multiplicado en los retratos:
otra vez Dios se disimula
bajo unos ojos amarillos
y Mao Tse-tung revistió
la túnica de los imperiales
y se coloca en un altar.

En vez de las flores que no
comenzaron nunca a nacer
se plantaron en los jardines
sus monumentales estatuas.
Sus oraciones reunidas
en un cuadernito escarlata
formaron el frasco infalible
de píldoras medicinales.
Lo cierto es que nadie mandó,
sino aquel hombre enmascarado.
Él otra vez pensó por todos.

Y sus palabras convertidas
en incantaciones sagradas
se repitieron hasta el mar

The truth is that clear
though it comes from the dark night.

The Worship (III)

But, once again, silence,
once again a face appears
forever without a smile
multiplied in the portraits:
God again disguises himself
behind yellow eyes
and Mao Tse-tung puts on
the tunic of the imperials
and places himself on the altar.

Instead of flowers that never
had a chance to be born,
his monumental statues
were planted in the gardens.
His speeches assembled
in a little red book
formed the infallible bottle
of medicinal pills.
The fact is, nobody gave orders,
only that masked man.
Again, he thought for everyone.

And his words converted
into sacred incantations
were repeated as far as the sea

por tantas bocas como arena,
por diez mil millones de lenguas.

LA LUZ

Siglo electrónico, tuviste
en tu frente pegado el ojo
de un nuevo dios que nos mataba
y que nos dictó la receta
de una salvación dolorosa!

Esto pasó cuando la olla
de los continentes ardía
y no servían los ejércitos:
no tenían a quién matar.

Una por una las regiones
extirpaban sus injusticias,
los pobres llegaban al pan,
se derramaba desde Cuba
la luz de los abecedarios
y a pesar de tantos pesares
crecía el sol en las escuelas.

Rusia elevó su torre insigne
sobre invasores castigados
y siguió trabajando el agua
por sus ríos horizontales
con más espacio cada día
en su estrella trabajadora.

by so many mouths like sand,
by ten billion tongues.

THE LIGHT

Electronic century, you had
stuck to your forehead the eye
of a new god who was killing us
and who dictated to us the prescription
for a painful salvation.

This happened when the pot
of the continents boiled over
and the armies no longer served:
they had no one left to kill.

One by one the regions
uprooted their injustices,
the poor reached the bread,
the light of the alphabets
spread outward from Cuba,
and in spite of so many sorrows
the sun bloomed in the schools.

Russia raised its famous tower
over the suffering invaders,
and the water labored on,
in her horizontal rivers
growing wider each day
on her hardworking star.

VIETNAM

Se llamaba Westmoreland
el inaudito estrangulante
que desde Washington llegó
a sembrar el padecimiento
en las entrañas vietnamesas,
pero fue extraño su destino:
sus propios muertos lo expulsaron
y ahora padece por su cuenta:
dejó para siempre a su patria
con las manos ensangrentadas.

De Vietnam salió un hilo oscuro
que fue amarrando nuestras vidas
a la lucha de aquel tan lejos,
un hilo de aguja tan cruel
que nos dolía y nos unía
dando vueltas al orbe amargo.
Será tal vez la última lucha
hecha por los pentagonales
en contra de los venideros?

Porque vivieron en el fuego
y murieron en la ceniza
los malvados de siempre ayer
y los heroicos de mañana:
los colonialistas manchados
por sus sinrazones perversas
y los defensores del reino
que llora en su cuna de sangre,
pero que nace cada día.

He was called Westmoreland
the obscure strangler
who arrived from Washington
to sow suffering
in Vietnamese entrails,
but his destiny was strange:
his own dead banished him,
and he suffers now on their account:
he forever forsook his motherland
with his bloodied hands.

From Vietnam a dark departed thread
that bound our lives
to the struggle so far away,
a thread of a needle so cruel
it hurt us and united us
spinning to the bitter orb.
Perhaps it will be the final struggle
waged by Pentagon troopers
against the future.

Because they lived in the fire
and died in the ash,
the wicked of forever yesterday
and the heroes of tomorrow:
the colonialists soiled
by their perverse wrongs
and the defenders of the kingdom
that cries in its cradle of blood,
yet that is born each day.

VII

Salí a encontrar lo que perdí
en las ciudades enemigas:
me cerraban calles y puertas,
me atacaban con fuego y agua,
me disparaban excrementos.
Yo sólo quería encontrar
juguetes rotos en los sueños,
un caballito de cristal
o mi reloj desenterrado.

Nadie quería comprender
mi melancólico destino,
mi desinterés absoluto.

En vano expliqué a las mujeres
que no quería robar nada,
ni asesinar a sus abuelas.
Daban gritos de miedo al ver
que yo salía de un armario
o entraba por la chimenea.

Sin embargo, por largos días
y noches de lluvia violeta
mantuve mis expediciones:
furtivamente atravesé
a través de techos y tejas
aquellas mansiones hostiles
y hasta debajo de la alfombra
luché y luché contra el olvido.

188

VII

The Seeker

I left to find what I lost
in enemy cities:
streets and doors closed on me,
they attacked me with fire and water,
they hurled shit at me.
I wanted only to find
broken toys in my dreams,
a small glass horse
or my exhumed clock.

No one wanted to understand
my melancholy destiny,
my absolute disinterest.

In vain I explained to women
that I was not out to steal anything,
nor to murder their grandmothers.
They screamed with fear at the sight
of me climbing from a cupboard
or entering through the chimney.

Still, through long days
and nights of violet rain
I made my expeditions:
furtively over the roofs and tiles
I crossed, passing through
those hostile mansions,
and even under the carpet
I fought and fought against forgetting.

Nunca encontré lo que buscaba.

Nadie tenía mi caballo,
ni mis amores, ni la rosa
que perdí como tantos besos
en la cintura de mi amada.

Fui encarcelado y malherido,
incomprendido y lesionado
como un malhechor evidente
y ahora no busco mi sombra.
Soy tan serio como los otros,
pero me falta lo que amé:
el follaje de la dulzura
que se desprende hoja por hoja
hasta que te quedas inmóvil,
verdaderamente desnudo.

MORIR

Cómo apartarse de uno mismo
(sin desconocerse tampoco):
abrir los cajones vacíos,
depositar el movimiento,
el aire libre, el viento verde,
y no dejar a los demás
sino una elección en la sombra,
una mirada en ascensor
o algún retrato de ojos muertos?

I never found what I was looking for.

No one had my horse,
or my loves, or my rose
I lost like so many kisses
on the waist of my beloved.

I was imprisoned, mistreated,
misunderstood and wounded
as a proven evildoer,
and I no longer seek my shadow.
I am as serious as the others,
but I miss what I loved:
the leaves of sweetness
that fall one by one
until you are ever motionless,
truly naked.

To Die

How does one separate from the self
(without forgetting oneself)—
by opening the empty boxes,
by storing movement within,
the free air, the green wind—
and not leave the others
save a choice in the shadows,
a look in an elevator,
or some portrait of dead eyes?

De alguna manera oficial
hay que establecer una ausencia
sin que haya nada establecido,
para que la curiosidad
sienta una ráfaga en la cara
cuando destapen la oratoria
y hallen debajo de los pies
la llamarada del ausente.

SIEMPRE YO

Yo que quería hablar del siglo
adentro de esta enredadera
que es mi siempre libro naciente,
por todas partes me encontré
y se me escapaban los hechos.
Con buena fe que reconozco
abrí los cajones al viento,
los armarios, los cementerios,
los calendarios con sus meses
y por las grietas que se abrían
se me aparecía mi rostro.

Por más cansado que estuviera
de mi persona inaceptable
volvía a hablar de mi persona
y lo que me parece peor
es que me pintaba a mí mismo
pintando un acontecimiento.

In some official way
one must establish an absence
without having established anything,
such that curiosity
feels a gust across the face
when they open the oratory
and discover under their feet
the flaring of the absent one.

I Always

I who wanted to speak of the century
within this bindweed
that is my book constantly budding,
I found myself everywhere
and facts escaped me.
With an honesty that I recognize
I opened the boxes to the wind,
the cupboards, the cemeteries,
the calendars with their months,
and in the widening cracks
appeared my face.

No matter how weary I was
of my unacceptable self,
I returned to speaking of myself,
and it seemed even worse to me
that I painted myself,
painting something happening.

Qué idiota soy dije mil veces
al practicar con maestría
las descripciones de mí mismo
como si no hubiera habido
nada mejor que mi cabeza,
nadie mejor que mis errores.

Quiero saber, hermanos míos,
dije en la Unión de Pescadores,
si todos se aman como yo.
La verdad es—me contestaron—
que nosotros pescamos peces
y tú te pescas a ti mismo
y luego vuelves a pescarte
y a tirarte al mar otra vez.

CONDICIONES

Con tantas tristes negativas
me despedí de los espejos
y abandoné mi profesión:
quise ser ciego en una esquina
y cantar para todo el mundo
sin ver a nadie porque todos
se me parecían un poco.

Pero buscaba mientras tanto
cómo mirarme hacia detrás,
hacia donde estaba sin ojos
y era oscura mi condición.
No saqué nada con cantar

What an idiot I am, I said a thousand times,
while practicing with mastery
descriptions of myself,
as though there had been
nothing better than my own head,
no one better than my mistakes.

I want to know, my brothers,
I said to the Fishermen's Union,
whether you all love yourselves as I do.
The truth is—they answered me—
we fish for fish
and you fish inside yourself
and later return to fish for yourself
and throw yourself back into the sea.

SITUATIONS

With so many sad denials
I said farewell to the mirrors
and I abandoned my profession:
I wanted to be blind on a corner
and sing for the whole world
without seeing anyone, because everyone
looked a little like me.

But all the while I was looking
for a way to see myself from behind
where I was without eyes
and my situation was dark.
I solved nothing by singing

como un ciego del populacho:
mientras más amarga la calle
me parecía yo más dulce.

Condenado a quererme tanto
me hice un hipócrita exterior
ocultando el amor profundo
que me causaban mis defectos.
Y así sigo siendo feliz
sin que jamás se entere nadie
de mi enfermedad insondable:
de lo que sufrí por amarme
sin ser, tal vez, correspondido.

ANDUVE

Solo con árboles y olor
a sauce mojado, es aún
tiempo de lluvia en el transcurso,
en la intemperie de Linares.

Hay un cielo central: más tarde
un horizonte abierto y húmedo
que se despliega y se desgarra
limpiando la naturaleza:

mas acá voy, desventurado,
sin tierra, sin cielo, remoto,
entre los labios colosales
de la soledad superior
y la indiferencia terrestre.

as a blind man of the masses:
while the street grew more bitter
it seemed I grew sweeter.

Condemned to like myself so much
I became outwardly hypocritical,
concealing the deep love
engendered by my faults.
And so I go on feeling happy
without anyone ever learning
of my unfathomable malady:
of the suffering I endured for loving myself
even as that love went unrequited.

I WALKED

Alone with trees and scent
of damp willow, it is still
the rainy season on the path,
in the wintry weather of Linares.

There is a central sky: later
a horizon open and humid
that spreads and rips,
scrubbing nature:

closer to here I travel, wretched,
without earth, without sky, remote,
between colossal lips
of highest solitude
and earthly indifference.

Oh antigua lluvia, ven y sálvame
de esta congoja inamovible!

RELÁMPAGO

Si fue una estrella innecesaria,
si de aquel fuego tembloroso
no quedó una huella encendida,
si se durmió el carbón oscuro
en la mina oscura del cielo,
no sé, no supe, no sabré.

Yo vi el fulgor de pez dorado
arriba, en la red que dejaba
caer sus gotas infinitas,
y luego perdí en las tinieblas
aquella inicial que temblaba
en el campamento celeste.

Dónde está, dije, crepitando
con su fuego comunicado,
dónde está la cítara verde?

Dónde se fue la llave ardiente?

Me sentí negro en la cintura
de la noche, negro y vacío
después de haber sido estrellado:
perdí la luz que se perdió
y por la noche intransigente
voló un aroma de humo amargo,

O ancient rain, come and save me
from everlasting anguish.

LIGHTNING

Whether it was an unnecessary star,
whether from that trembling fire
no fiery footprint remained,
whether the dark coal fell asleep
in the dark mine of the sky,
I do not know, did not know, never will know.

I saw the blaze of golden fish
high up, in the net that let
fall its infinite drops,
and later I lost in the darkest dark
that initial that shivered
in the encampment of stars.

Where is it, I asked, crackling
with its communicated fire,
where is the green zither?

Where did the burning key go?

I felt black around the waist
of the night, black and empty,
after having been riddled with stars:
I lost the light that was lost
and through the uncompromising night
an aroma of bitter smoke spread

como si el mundo se quemara
en alguna parte del cielo
y se me apagaran los ojos
en la iniquidad del silencio.

VOLVER VOLVIENDO

Sacude el camino cortando
heroicas flores amarillas
y sigue apartando los cerros
abriendo el cielo a borbotones:
voy hacia lejos otra vez,
a la humedad enmarañada
de las cumbres de Nahuelbuta
y en el titánico transcurso
crece en mi ropa la distancia
y me voy haciendo camino.

Atravesando cordilleras
sin saber cómo se afiló
mi frente longitudinal
y saqué los pies de la tierra
para que no fueran raíces,
sino festín del movimiento.

El día izquierdo olvidará
la rosa rápida y perdida
antes de ser inaugurada,
porque debo llegar temprano
a mis lejanas circunstancias,
a saber lo que deja el río

as if the world were burning
in some part of the sky,
and my eyes burned out
in the iniquity of silence.

To Return Returning

The cutting path shakes
heroic yellow flowers
and goes on parting the hills
opening the sky to boiling:
once again I go farther,
to the tangled humidity
of the peaks of Nahuelbuta,
and on that titanic course
distance grows in my clothes
and I leave blazing a trail.

Crossing mountain ranges
without knowing how,
my longitudinal brow grew pointed
and I yanked my feet from the earth
so they would not become roots,
but instead a feast of motion.

The left-leaning day will forget
the rapid and lost rose
before being inaugurated,
because I must arrive early
at my distant circumstances,
to know what the river deposits

en la insistencia de la orilla
con tantas palabras de piedra
como los pelos de un caballo.

La carretera corre abajo
hacia tal vez, hacia Coyhaique,
donde el agua se desarrolla
como el violín en un lamento.
Y tengo patria más allá
donde corre el avestruz verde
contra las ráfagas navales
y comienza el reino sin dioses
donde el hielo es la claridad.

SEX

Se abrió tal vez el gineceo
en el año de nuestros años
y el sexo saltó las ventanas,
los ministerios y las puertas,
y vimos asomar los senos
en la celeste timidez
de las tarjetas postales
hasta que sobre el escenario
se deshojaron las mujeres
y una ola inmensa de desnudos
sobrepasó las catedrales.

Luego el comercio estableció
con libros, pantallas, revistas,
el imperio inmenso del culo

at the insistence of the bank,
with as many words of stone
as are hairs on a horse.

The road runs below
toward maybe, toward Coyhaique,
where the water unfurls
like the violin in a lament.
And I have motherland beyond
where the green ostrich runs
against the nautical gusts
and the kingdom without gods begins
where the ice is clarity.

SEX

Maybe the pistils opened
in the year of our years
and sex broke the windows,
the ministries and the doors,
and we saw the breasts appear
in the starry shyness
of the postcards
until on stage
women lost their leaves
and an immense wave of nakedness
broke over the cathedrals.

Then commerce established
with books, lampshades, magazines,
the vast empire of the ass,

hasta inundar las poblaciones
con esperma industrializada.

Era difícil escapar
hacia el amor o tus trabajos,
te perseguían los ladridos
del sexo desencadenado
depositado en almacenes,
chorreando gotas mensajeras,
alcanzándote en los anuncios,
siguiéndote en la carretera
o regando hasta las aldeas
con su acueducto genital.

La literatura cruzó
este siglo de falo en falo
haciendo graciosas piruetas
o cayéndose de agonía
y los libros que se ensuciaron
no cayeron en otra charca
que la del alma malherida.

Sépase que sin jardinero
fue más bello el jardín hirsuto,
pero una negra enredadera
enrolló su pelo de espanto
en los libros de la desdicha.

Y así fue la página blanca,
que se parecía a la luna,
transformándose en patrimonio
de una tristísima impudicia,
hasta que no tuvimos libros
para leer sino la luz

flooding whole countries
with industrialized sperm.

It was difficult to escape
into love or your work—
they persecuted you, the growls
of sex unleashed,
deposited in warehouses,
messenger drops dripping,
reaching you with advertisements,
following you on the road
or bathing even the villages
with its genital aqueduct.

Literature made its way
in this century phallus by phallus
by performing amusing pirouettes
or falling in agony,
and the books that soiled themselves
fell into a single pond,
that of the wicked soul.

Let it be known that without a gardener
the shaggy garden was more lovely,
but black bindweed
unfurled its frightful hair
in the books of our misfortune.

And so did the blank page,
which resembled the moon
rendering itself in its heritage
of such sad shamelessness,
until we had no books
to read other than the light,

y cinco sílabas de sol
son una palabra desnuda
y la razón de la pureza.

BOMBA (II)

Y no estoy seguro del mar
en este día presuntuoso:
tal vez los peces se vistieron
con las escamas nucleares
y adentro del agua infinita
en vez del frío original
crecen los fuegos de la muerte.

Se empeñan en poblar de espanto
las bruscas mareas del mundo
y no hay torre que nos ampare
de tantas olas enemigas.

No se contentan con la tierra.

Hay que asesinar el océano.

Con algunas gotas de infierno
se mezcla la sal de las olas
y se descargan al abismo
los minerales de la cólera,
hasta batir la tempestad
en una taza de veneno
y servir al hombre la sopa
de fuego de mar y de muerte.

and five syllables of sun
are a naked word
and the source of purity.

BOMB (II)

I am no longer sure of the sea
in this presumptuous day:
perhaps the fish dressed
themselves in nuclear scales,
and within the infinite water
instead of the original cold
grow the fires of death.

They commit to colonizing with fear,
the sudden tides of the world,
and no tower can protect us
from so many enemy waves.

They are not content with the earth.

They need to murder the ocean.

With a few drops of hell
the salt of the waves mingle,
and the minerals of fury
are discharged in the abyss,
so that they whip up the tempest
in a cup of poison
and serve mankind the soup
of fire of sea and of death.

VIII

La cierta luz de un día tiene
alas tan duras y seguras
que se derrochan en la rosa:
parece que van a morir:
parece que tantos anillos
sobran a los dedos del día:
parece que no vuelve a arder
otro reloj con esta esfera:
hay demasiada claridad
para mi pequeño planeta.

No es así, lo sabe la tierra
en su mojada intimidad.
Los minerales recibieron
noticias que reverberaban
y el átomo cristalizó
un movimiento de relámpago.

Yo asumo este día delgado
como una cinta alrededor
de la tristeza circundante
y me hago un cinturón, un vaso,
un buque para transmigrar,
un océano de rocío.

Vengan a ver sobre la abeja
una cítara de platino,
sobre la cítara la miel

VIII

The certain light of a day has
wings so durable and sure
they are wasted on the rose:
it seems they are going to die:
it seems the fingers of the day
have far too many rings:
it seems another clock with this face
is not burning again:
there is too much clarity
for my small planet.

It is not so, the earth knows
in its moist intimacy.
The minerals received
reverberating news
and the atom crystallized
how the lightning moves.

I take the form of this slender day
like a round ribbon
of surrounding sadness
and I become a belt, a glass,
a ship passing from one body to another
an ocean of dew.

Come see on the bee
a zither of platinum,
on the zither the honey,

y sobre la miel la cintura
de mi amorosa transparente.

Me pasé la vida en la dicha
y en la desdicha me pasé
toda mi vida y otras vidas,
por eso en este día azul
he convidado a todo el mundo.

No me saluden al entrar,
pero no me insulten tampoco.

Soy un pequeño profesor:
doy clases de luz a la tierra.

PUNTA DEL ESTE 1968

Sin saberlo vengo a llegar,
vengo llegando el mismo día
a la misma punta del día
y se repite mi recuerdo
con el contenido fragante
que tuvo el tiempo de otro tiempo.
Aquí está el mismo sol caído
sobre las dunas y las olas
y el aire que rompe las púas
de las hostiles bromeliáceas.
Por fin después de navegar
llego adonde yo me esperaba.

and on the honey the waist
of my transparent love.

I spent my life in happiness
and in unhappiness I spent
my whole life and other lives,
which is why on this blue day
I have invited the whole world.

Do not wave at me when I come in,
but do not insult me, either.

I am an obscure professor:
I teach classes of light to the earth.

PUNTA DEL ESTE, 1968

Without knowing it I happen to arrive,
I happen to arrive the same day,
at the same point of the day,
and my memory returns
with the fragrant contents
whose time was of another time.
Here is the same sun fallen
over the dunes and the waves
and the air that smashes the thorns
of the hostile bromeliads.
Finally, after sailing around,
I arrived where I expected to.

Es Olga la que se sentó
hace diez años en su silla
cuando Alberto se descalzó
en honor de las golondrinas.
Es claro que las dracaemas
proclamaron nuevas espadas
y la glicina derramó
su color de idilio perfecto.
(Supongamos que pasó el tiempo
en el corazón del copihue
y en la patria de Lautréamont,
y que además tanques y huelgas
convocaron nuestros dolores
agregando arrepentimiento
a la copa de cada día.)

Pero la verdad que es idéntico
el aquel pasado con éste
y que descansa la razón
cuando se repite el pasado.

No nos queremos desdichar.

Todas las citas escondieron
uno que otro o muchos lamentos:
es estática la alegría:
es azul el fuego del cielo:
a pesar de todos sus ojos
es ciega la noche estrellada.

Vengo a vivir lo que viví
aunque sea una gota de agua

Olga is the one who sat
in her chair ten years ago
when Alberto took off his shoes
in honor of the swallows.
It is clear that the dracaena
heralded new swords
and the wisteria spilled
its color of perfect idyll.
(We are assuming that time passed
in the heart of the Chilean bellflower
and in the motherland of Lautréamont,
and also that tanks and strikes
rallied our sadnesses,
gathering up regrets
in the wineglass of each day.)

But the truth is, that past
is identical to this past,
and reason takes a nap
when the past repeats itself.

We do not like being unhappy.

All the appointments concealed
one or more or many laments:
joy is static:
the fire of the sky is blue:
despite all its eyes
the starry night is blind.

I come to live what I lived
though I am a drop of water

o la cintura de la arena,
los pinos de Punta del Este
o una camiseta morada.
Yo te regalo dos pistolas
si eres más valiente que yo
o por lo menos más difícil:
avanzar volviendo a partir:
dormir cada vez más despierto.

JANEIRO

Dejadme este vago esplendor
de una ciudad, de una distancia
que brille en mí como el recuerdo
de una luciérnaga en la mano:
tal vez Río centelleando
como una enorme mariposa
de precisión fosforescente
o tal vez São Paulo establece
la azucena rectangular
de su vertical estructura
o Brasilia con su fulgor
de diamante deshabitado
nos hicieron vivir mañana,
nos enseñaron a después.

Pero son los densos designios
de vegetales derramados
o las anchas aguas que fluyen
por el espacio brasilero
o el olor a goma salvaje

or waist of the sand,
the pines of Punta del Este
or a purple T-shirt.
I hand you two pistols
whether you are braver than me
or simply more difficult:
advancing to leave once more:
sleeping, each time more awake.

JANEIRO

Leave me this faint splendor
of a city, of a distance
that might shine in me like the memory
of a firefly in the hand:
perhaps Rio sparkling
like an enormous butterfly
of phosphorescent precision,
or perhaps São Paulo erects
the rectangular Madonna lily
of its vertical structure,
or Brasília with its shine
of uninhabited diamond
moved us to live another day,
and later showed us how.

But they are the dense designs
of spilled vegetables
or the wide waters flowing
through the vastness of Brazil
or the smell of gum

del fondo, o las bestias durmiendo
en la somnolencia mojada
o el linaje negro en la orilla
del baile, cerca de la espuma,
o arriba en Bahía sonora
con el sortilegio macumbo
o la sacrílega sonata
de las favelas desdentadas
o el vaho negro del café
o la insigne pajarería
o las cascadas desplomando
la torre de las esmeraldas,
la lengua del oso hormiguero
con la muchedumbre adhesiva
del crecimiento pululante,
pero más que el vestido verde
o la voz loca del turpial
es el espacioso silencio,
el patrimonio imperturbado,
el que me visita en mis sueños:
oh Brasil, brasero brutal
que calla encendido en su brasa,
en su placenta planetaria,
como si siguiera naciendo
sin voz, sin ojos todavía,
corriendo inmóvil sin llegar,
edificando sin nacer,
comenzando toda la luz
sin separarse de la sombra.

wild to the core, or the sleeping beasts
in the damp somnolence
or the black lineage along the shore
of the dance, near the foam,
or up there in sonorous Bahia,
with the macumba sorcery
or the sacrilegious sonata
of the toothless shantytowns
or the black steam of the café
or the famous bird shop
or the waterfalls toppling
the tower of emeralds,
the tongue of the anteater
with the sticking throng
of swarming growth,
but greater than the green dress
or the crazy voice of the turpial
is the vast silence,
the undisturbed heritage,
the one who visits me in my dreams:
Oh, Brazil, brutal brazier
that remains quietly lit in its ember,
in its planetary placenta
as though it would go on being born
without a voice, still without eyes,
running in place and never arriving,
building without being born,
kindling the light
without separating from shadow.

Venezuela

Por Caracas dura y desnuda
y sus alturas matorrales
anduve, loco de vivir,
ahíto de luz, atropellado
por la salud de Venezuela.

Enarbolada por la luz
entre los verdes masteleros
recorre la estatua yacente
una burbuja de petróleo
que concurre por las arterias
al corazón electoral.

Yo soy el bardo que cantó
la trinitaria afirmación
de sus pájaros encendidos,
porque no hay canto que no canten
los frenéticos cantarines
y no hay fulgor que no inauguren
los voladores venezuelos.

Retrato de una mujer

Se llamaba Caramelaria,
era rosada de costumbres,
iba con besos deliciosos
que se le caían del pelo,
de las caderas, de la boca,

VENEZUELA

Through hard and naked Caracas
and her high thickets
I walked, crazy about living,
full of light, stricken
by the health of Venezuela.

Hoisted by the light
between green topmasts,
the recumbent statue travels
through a bubble of petroleum
that passes through the arteries
to the electoral heart.

I am the bard who sang
the trinitarian affirmation
of its fiery red birds,
there is no song
those frenetic singers do not sing
and no splendor not inaugurated by
the flying fish of Venezuela.

PORTRAIT OF A WOMAN

She was called Caramelaria,
she was peach pink in her ways,
she traveled with delicious kisses
that fell from her hair,
from her hips, from her mouth,

era completamente azul
aquella mujer amarilla.

Yo la perdí con avidez
en el otoño ceniciento,
cuando a causa de mis dolores
me preparé para partir.
Llorando con todos los ojos
me acomodé en mi bicicleta.

Qué tiempo remoto cubierto
por el polen de su contacto,
por los metales de su ausencia!

Edifiqué mi alegoría
pensando en sus pámpanas piernas,
en su corazón de coral,
en sus uñas alimenticias.

Yo soy aquel que desertó
en plena vigencia del viento
desamparando mi tristeza
hasta que la soledad
me enseñó a mirar las manzanas,
a dar la mano al coronel,
a entenderme con las palmeras.

Voy a tratar de describir
aquellos acontecimientos,
aquel reino adonde llegué
sin un perro que me ladrara:
aquel castillo enharinado
devorado por las abejas

she was completely blue
that yellow woman.

I greedily lost her
in the ashen autumn,
when because of my pain
I prepared myself to leave her.
Crying with all my eyes,
I climbed on my bicycle.

What a distant time, coated
with the pollen of her touch,
with the metals of her absence!

I constructed my allegory
thinking about her tendril-like legs,
about her heart of coral,
about her nourishing nails.

I am the one who deserted
with the full force of the wind,
forsaking my sadnesses
until my solitude
taught me to pay heed to the apples,
to shake hands with the colonel,
to get along with the palm trees.

I am going to try describing
these events,
the kingdom where I arrived
and no dog would bark at me:
that castle covered in flour
devoured by the bees,

en que viví sin asomarme
a ninguna ventana, nunca.

NACIMIENTOS

Voy a contarles cómo nace
un volcán en la tierra mía:
en Paricutín o Chillán,
me da lo mismo, buenas gentes:
las tribus no saben de cercos
y no se divide el verano.

Antes de alzarse hay un vacío
como de luz recién lavada
y luego llega el terciopelo
a participar en las flores
hasta que una cinta delgada
de vapor con color de luna
comienza a brotar de una piedra:
se abrió la boca de la tierra.

Se abre la boca de la tierra
y se delinea un embudo,
un seno de mujer de arcilla,
algo que crece y que se mueve
como potro o locomotora
exhalando el acre vahído
de una sulfúrica cerveza
que quiere arder y desbordar
desde su copa subterránea.

in which I lived never looking out
of any window, not ever.

BIRTHS

I am going to tell them how a volcano
is born in my land:
in Paricutín or Chillán,
it's all the same to me, good people:
the tribes know nothing about fences
and summer does not separate itself.

Before rising, there is an emptiness
as of light recently rinsed
and later the velvet arrives,
taking part among the flowers
until a fine stream
of steam the color of the moon
begins to sprout from a stone:
the mouth of the earth opened.

The mouth of the earth opens
and a funnel forms,
a breast of a woman of clay,
something that grows and moves
like a colt or a locomotive
exhaling the acrid dizziness
of a sulfuric beer
that wants to burn and brim over
in its subterranean glass.

Milagro es ahora el silencio
mientras crece el monte del fuego
hasta que estallan las espadas
y toda la ferretería:
cuelgan los panales calientes
y las abejas del infierno,
crepitan y caen subiendo
las cenizas de la montaña.

Los truenos que vienen de abajo
no son los mismos del cielo:
son carcajadas con azufre,
son alegrías enterradas,
y ruge subiendo el volcán
como si saliera a jugar
con la dicha y la llamarada.

Ya nació, ya mide milímetros,
ya tiene su nube en la punta
como un pañuelo en la nariz.
Ya tiene derecho a crecer:
preocupémonos del maíz
porque aquí no ha pasado nada.

CANCIÓN CON PAISAJE Y RÍO

De Villarrica los collados,
los rectángulos amarillos,
la fiesta verde horizontal,
las fucsias de boca violeta
además del último orgullo

Miraculous now is the silence
as the mountain of fire grows
until the swords explode
and the whole ironworks:
the hot honeycombs
and the bees of hell,
they crackle and fall, climbing
the ashes of the mountain.

The thunderclaps that come from below
are not the same as from the sky:
they are bursts of laughter with sulfur,
they are buried joys,
and the volcano roars, climbing
as though it were coming out to play
with happiness and flaring.

It was already born, it already measures millimeters,
it already has a cloud at its peak
like a handkerchief on the nose.
It already has the right to grow:
let us busy ourselves with the corn
because here nothing has happened.

SONG WITH COUNTRYSIDE AND RIVER

From Villarrica the hills,
the yellow rectangles,
the green horizontal festivities,
the fuchsias with their violet mouths,
not to mention the utmost pride

de los robles sobrevivientes:
voy entrando en mi propia edad,
en las aguas que me nacieron.

A mí me dio a luz el galope
de la lluvia entre los terrones
y nunca pude abrir los ojos
de par en par, como es debido:

yo me quedé semienterrado
como la simiente olvidada
y jugué con la oscuridad
sin olvidar los buenos días.

Ahora que se reintegran
a estas soledades mis huesos
varias veces vuelvo a nacer
por arte del sol tempestuoso,
hundo en el pasto la cabeza,
tocan el cielo mis raíces.

A Villarrica por el río
Toltén Toltén Toltén Toltén.

PUERTOS

Olor rabioso de pescado
hay en las puertas del puerto:
un olor sucio y sombrío
como un invierno envenenado,
atacado por la gangrena.

of the surviving oak trees:
I am entering my own era,
in the waters that gave birth to me.

What birthed me was the galloping
of the rain among lumps of earth,
and I was not able to open my eyes
wide, as is proper:

I remained half buried
like the forgotten seed
and played with the darkness,
without forgetting the good days.

Now that my bones
rejoin these solitudes
I, at various times, am born again
through the art of the stormy sun,
I sink my head in the pasture,
my roots touch the sky.

To Villarrica by the river
Toltén Toltén Toltén Toltén.

PORTS

Rabid odor of fish
at the doors of the port:
a dirty and somber odor
like a poisoned winter,
attacked by gangrene.

Son los vestigios de la vida.

Son los rayos de la pobreza.

Ay la pobre patria arrugó
sus viejos párpados de nieve
y se sentó a llorar, tal vez
en los polvorientos andenes,
en los malecones del Sur,
cerca de las pescaderías.

Sentada ve correr el agua
de las tenebrosas acequias,
el detritus del arrabal,
las agallas asesinadas
y los rígidos gatos muertos.

Un color de naranja y nieve
tenía la patria en los libros
y por el pelo le caía
una cascada de cerezas.
Por eso da pena mirarla
sentada en una silla rota
entre las cáscaras de papas
y los muebles desvencijados.

En las puertas rotas del puerto
se oye el lamento abrumador
de un remolcador moribundo.
Y la noche cae de bruces
como un saco negro de harapos
en las rodillas de la patria.

They are shards of life.

They are rays of poverty.

Oh, poor mother country screwed up
her old eyelids of snow
and sat down to cry, perhaps
on dusty station platforms,
on the jetties of the South,
near the fish markets.

Seated, she sees the flowing water
of the dark irrigation ditches,
the detritus of the outskirts,
the assassinated gills,
and the stiff dead cats.

In the books, mother country
was the color of oranges and snow,
and through her hair fell
a cascade of cherries.
So it hurts to see her
seated in a broken chair,
among potato peelings
and rickety furniture.

In the broken doors of the port
the overwhelming lament
of a dying tugboat is heard.
And the night falls on its face
like a black sack of rags
over the knees of mother country.

IX

REGRESANDO

A diez días de viaje largo
y desprovisto de opiniones
vuelvo a mi ser, a ser yo mismo,
el societario solitario
que pide siempre la palabra
para retener el derecho
de quedarse luego callado.

Resulta que llego otra vez
al centro inmóvil de mí mismo
desde donde nunca salí
y como en un reloj dormido
veo la hora verdadera:
la que se detiene una vez
no para inducir a la muerte,
sino para abrirte la vida.

Sucede que me moví tanto
que mis huesos se despertaban
en pleno sueño, caminando
hacia arrabales que crucé,
mercados que me sostuvieron,
escuelas que me perseguían,
aviones bajo la tormenta,
plazas llenas de gente urgente
y sobre mi alma que sin duda
se puso a dormir su fatiga
mi cuerpo continuó los viajes

IX

Ten days into a long journey
and with an utter lack of opinions
I return to my self, to being myself,
the solitary union member
who always requests the floor
so as to retain the right
to later keep quiet.

It turns out that I arrive again
at the motionless center of myself
from where I never departed,
and as on a sleeping clock
I see the honest hour:
one that stops this once
so as not to lead to death,
but to open you up to life.

I happened to move so much
my bones awakened
in fullest dream, walking
toward outskirts that I crossed,
markets that sustained me,
schools that chased me,
planes sitting in the storm,
plazas full of hurrying people,
and over my soul that without a doubt
put its weariness to bed
my body continued its journeys

con la vibración trepidante
de un camión repleto de piedras
que machacaba mi esqueleto.

A ver, alma, resucitemos
el punto en que se saludaron
el horario y el minutero:
ésa es la rendija del tiempo
para salir de la desdicha
y penetrar en la frescura.

(Allí hay un estanque infinito
hecho con láminas iguales
de transcurso y de transparencia
y no necesito mover
los cinco dedos de una mano
para recoger mis dolores
o la naranja prometida.)

De tanto volver a ese punto
comprendí que no necesito
tantos caminos para andar,
ni tantas sílabas externas,
ni tantos hombres ni mujeres,
ni tantos ojos para ver.

Parece—yo no lo aseguro—
que basta con ese minuto
que se detiene y precipita
lo que llevabas inconcluso
y no importa tu perfección,
ni tu ansiedad diseminada

with the trembling vibration
of a truck full of stones
which crushed my bones.

Let's see, soul, let's resuscitate
the moment they saluted,
the hour hand and the minute hand:
that is the crack in time
by which to leave misfortune
and enter the freshness.

(There, there is an infinite reservoir
made of sheets
equal in transparency
and the passing of time,
and I do not need to move
the five fingers of a hand
to gather my sadnesses
or the promised orange.)

From so often returning to this moment
I understood that I do not need
so many paths to walk,
nor so many external syllables,
nor so many men or women,
nor so many eyes to see.

It seems—I am not sure of it—
that no more is needed than this single minute
that stops and speeds up
the unfinished things you carried,
and your perfection is of no importance,
nor is your anxiety scattered

en polvorientos derroteros:
basta con bajar a ver
el silencio que te esperaba
y sientes que van a llegarte
las tentaciones del otoño,
las invitaciones del mar.

PRENSA

Contemplé la edad de papel
vestida de hojas amarillas
que poco a poco sumergieron
la superficie de la tierra:

un periodismo matorral
encendió incendios alevosos
o mató con una mentira
o propagó desodorantes
o confitó las tiranías
o difundió la oscuridad.

Cada periódico propuso
las leyes de su propietario
y se vendieron las noticias
rociadas con sangre y veneno.

La guerra esperaba sentada
leyendo los diarios del mundo
desde sus órbitas sin ojos.
Y yo escuché cómo reía
con sus mandíbulas amargas

along dusty seafaring routes:
it is enough to sink down to see
the silence that awaited you
and you feel they will gather you up,
the temptations of autumn,
the invitations of the sea.

PRINTING PRESS

I contemplated the age of paper
dressed in yellow leaves
that little by little covered
the surface of the earth:

a scrub journalism
ignited treacherous fires
or killed with a lie
or spread deodorant
or preserved tyrannies in syrup
or broadcast the darkness.

Each newspaper affirmed
the laws of its owner
and the news was sold
sprinkled with blood and poison.

The war was waiting, seated,
reading the dailies of the world
with its sockets and no eyes.
And I listened to how it laughed
with its bitter jaws,

leyendo los editoriales
que la trataban con ternura.

El hombre de piedra pasó
a ser el hombre de papel,
vestido por fuera y por dentro
con pasiones prefabricadas
o con tapiz intestinal.

El sexo y la sangre llenaron
todas las páginas del mundo
y era difícil encontrar
una jovencita desnuda
comiéndose una manzana
junto al agua de un río azul,
porque los ríos se llenaron
de tinta tétrica de imprenta
y el viento cubrió de periódicos
las ciudades y los volcanes.

EL ENEMIGO

Hoy vino a verme un enemigo.
Se trata de un hombre encerrado
en su verdad, en su castillo,
como en una caja de hierro,
con su propia respiración
y las espaldas singulares
que amamantó para el castigo.

reading the editorials
that treated it with tenderness.

The man of stone became
the man of paper,
dressed on the outside and the inside
with prefabricated passions
or an intestinal tapestry.

Sex and blood filled
the pages of the world,
and it was hard to find
a young naked girl
eating an apple
beside the water of a blue river,
because the rivers were filled
with sullen ink of the presses,
and the wind covered with newspaper
the cities and the volcanoes.

THE ENEMY

Today an enemy came to see me.
This is a man locked
in his truth, in his castle,
as in an iron box,
with his own breath
and his singular swords
that he suckled as punishment.

Miré los años en su rostro,
en sus ojos de agua cansada,
en las líneas de soledad
que le subieron a las sienes
lentamente, desde el orgullo.

Hablamos en la claridad
de un medio día pululante,
con viento que esparcía sol
y sol combatiendo en el cielo.
Pero el hombre sólo mostró
las nuevas llaves, el camino
de todas las puertas. Yo creo
que adentro de él iba el silencio
que no podía compartirse.
Tenía una piedra en el alma:
él preservaba la dureza.

Pensé en su mezquina verdad
enterrada sin esperanza
de herir a nadie sino a él
y miré mi pobre verdad
maltratada adentro de mí.

Allí estábamos cada uno
con su certidumbre afilada
y endurecida por el tiempo
como dos ciegos que defienden
cada uno su oscuridad.

I saw the years in his face,
in his eyes of weary water,
in the lines of loneliness
that climbed to his temples
slowly, from his pride.

We spoke in the clarity
of a swarming noon
with wind scattering sunlight,
and sunlight battling in the sky.
But the man merely held out
the new keys, the pathway
to all the doors. I believe
that within he was silence,
unable to share himself.
He had a stone in his soul:
he was keeping the hardness.

I thought about his paltry truth
buried with no hope whatsoever
of hurting anyone but himself,
and I watched my poor truth
treated poorly inside of me.

There we were, each of us
with his sharp conviction
and hardened by time
like two blind men defending
each other's darkness.

No se trata de perdonar:
el perdonado no perdona.
Tampoco se trata de dar
porque el que recibe recuerda
como una herida tu bondad.

Entonces, de qué se nutrió,
yo te pregunto, tu alegría?
Por dónde salieron tus ojos
sin que no los acribillaran?
Qué razón para sonreír
y qué viento para bailar
y qué contacto para siempre
y con qué perdura tu canto?
Adentro del puño la espina
te hiere para defenderte
y pesa la piedra en tu mano
o el revólver en tu desvelo.

Así, pues, no matas a nadie
cuando todos te están matando
como si tuvieras repuesto
para la vida que te matan,
porque las armas son pesadas
o las palabras son azules
o porque no debes bajar
cuando no quisiste subir
o porque no existen, te dicen,
los que patean tu cabeza
o porque los proliferantes
se irán a proliferar

THE FIST AND THE THORN

It is not about forgiving:
the forgiven does not forgive,
nor is it about giving
because he who receives
remembers your kindness as a wound.

On what did it feed,
I ask you, your joy?
Where did your eyes emerge
if they didn't poke them into you?
What makes one smile
and the wind dance
and a touch last
and on what does your song subsist?
Inside the fist the thorn
wounds you to defend you
and the stone weighs heavy in your hand
or the revolver in your insomnia.

So, then, you do not kill anyone
when everyone is killing you
as though you had provisions
for the life they kill,
because the weapons are heavy
or the words are blue,
or because you must not descend
when you refused to ascend,
or because they do not exist, they tell you,
those who stomp on your head
or because those who proliferate
will leave to proliferate

o porque ocultas el orgullo
como un dragón de siete suelas
o porque te sientes culpable
de haber nacido, de crecer,
de comprar uvas en la tienda,
de desistir y de llegar.

Por estas variadas razones
—o simplemente de tristeza—
enrollas el mal que te hicieron,
recoges las piedras del daño,
y te vas silbando y silbando
por la mañana y por la arena.

COLONIANDO

Este siglo fue devolviendo
aquellas tierras devoradas
por las centurias anteriores
y fue un espectáculo abierto
ver imperiales señoríos
vomitando con parsimonia
independencias engullidas,
oscuras banderas tragadas,
naciones negras o amarillas,
razas de reinos consumidos.

Otras veces, a tiro limpio,
Congos cargados de metralla
o vietnameses insurrectos
quebrantaron el protocolo:

or because you hide your pride
like a dragon of seven soles
or because if you are guilty
it's guilty of having been born, of growing,
of buying grapes at the store,
of giving up and of arriving.

For these myriad reasons
—or simply from sadness—
you coil up the evil they inflicted on you,
you gather up the stones of the damage done,
and you leave whistling and whistling
in the morning and across the sand.

COLONIZING

This century was returning
those lands devoured
by previous centuries,
and it was a spectacle
to see imperial lords
vomiting with frugality
gobbled-up freedoms,
dark swallowed flags,
black and yellow nations,
races of consumed kingdoms.

At other times, guns blazing,
Congolese, weighed down by shrapnel,
or Vietnamese rebels
violated the protocol:

los que ya sabían morir
pronto aprendieron a matar.

Java, donde me fui a vivir
adolescente y casadero,
acribilló a sus coloniales
y las tres mil islas ardieron:
se incendiaron los arrozales
y se llenaron de rubíes
los templos de piedra dorada
cuando bailaron los relámpagos
de los *krisses* ondulatorios.

Ceilán que amé cambió de luz,
brilló como un panal marino
y sus palmeras crepitaron.

Fue vaporoso el medio siglo
con las colonias reventando
como negras frutas podridas
en la esclavitud del sudor.

Las manos que fueron cortadas
a comienzos de nuestra edad
se reintegraron a los cuerpos
de los callados insepultos
o de furiosos moribundos
y África se sacudió
como un elefante incendiado
en una bodega infernal.

Salieron los últimos belgas,
escoceses de última hora,

those who already knew how to die
quickly learned how to kill.

Java, where I went to live
not yet mature and of marrying age,
machine-gunned its colonizers
and three thousand islands burned:
the rice fields caught fire
and the temples of golden stone
filled with rubies
when danced the lightning
of the undulating *kerisses.*

Ceylon, which I loved, changed light,
shined like a honeycomb of the sea,
and its palm trees crackled.

The middle of the century was steamy
with the colonies bursting
like black fruit rotting
in the slavery of sweat.

The hands that were severed
at the beginning of our era
reunited with the bodies
of those silent and unburied
or of those raging as they die,
and while Africa shuddered
like an elephant on fire
in an infernal cellar.

The last Belgians left,
the last-minute Scotsmen,

y adentro de la oscuridad
en su silencio sanguinario
Salazar siguió encadenando
los brazos oscuros de Angola,
hasta que la muerte llegó
a sentarse a su cabecera
atormentándolo por fin:
devolviéndole sus tormentos.

En estas horas en que escribo
aún agoniza Salazar
y pido con tacto a la muerte,
con humildad, con cortesía,
que no lo mate todavía.
De esta manera, en este punto
escribo mi ruego a la muerte.

Mátalo, Muerte, lentamente:
que primero derrame un ojo,
que guarden ese ojo podrido
en un orinal o un tintero
y que Salazar se lo trague
con un aliño de alfileres.

Muerte, te ruego que confundas
sus fríos hígados de hiena
con una pelota de fútbol
que, sin que lo sepa el tirano,
sin desprenderse de su cuerpo,
sirva a los negros de juguete
en la cancha hirsuta de Angola.

and inside the darkness
in his bloodthirsty silence
Salazar remained shackled
to the dark arms of Angola,
until death arrived
to sit at the head of his bed
torturing him ceaselessly:
repaying his tortures.

In these hours in which I write
Salazar is still dying
and I politely ask death,
with humility, with tact,
not to kill him just yet.
In this way, at this time
I write my request to death.

Kill him, Death, slowly:
first pour out an eye,
then keep that rotten eye
in a chamber pot or an inkwell
and make Salazar swallow it,
seasoned with pins.

Death, I request that you conflate
his cold guts of hyena
with a soccer ball
that, without the tyrant knowing it,
without him leaving his body,
serves as a plaything for the black sportsmen
on the shaggy field of Angola.

Te pido, Muerte, que sus pies
conserven fragmentos sensibles
y sean quemados a pausa
en la salsa que sus orejas
dejen caer a goterones
derritiéndose en el infierno,
en el infierno que el tirano
emprendió para sus suplicios.

Muerte, entrega sin vacilar
a las hormigas africanas
los testículos del tirano:
que los testículos resecos
sean mordidos y comidos
por insectos devoradores.

Es demasiado

Hoy me parece que sostengo
todo el cielo con mis anteojos
y que la tierra no se mueve
debajo de mis pies pesados.
Sucede al hombre y a su estirpe
sentirse crecer falsamente
y falsamente destinarse
una falsa soberanía!

Así se levanta a sí mismo
una cabeza colosal
y se siente grande por dentro,
por la izquierda y por la derecha,

I beg you, Death, may his feet
retain bits of feeling
and be leisurely burned
in the sauce that his ears
let fall in big drops,
melting in hell,
in the hell on which the tyrant
embarked for his tortures.

Death, do not hesitate to leave
for African ants
the testicles of the tyrant:
so those dried-up testicles
are bitten and eaten
by devouring insects.

It Is Too Much

Today it seems I am holding up
the whole sky with my eyeglasses
and the earth does not shift
under my heavy feet.
It dogs a man and his ancestry,
what it is to grow falsely
and falsely intend to assume
a false sovereignty!

So, it rises to itself
a colossal head,
it feels huge inside,
on the left and on the right

a la distancia y de perfil,
y por delante y por detrás.

Se busca el escritor creciente
un crítico color de mosca
que le dore cada domingo
su pildorita de moda.
Pero no menos le sucede
al militar inoportuno
que comanda y comanda números
y regimientos de papel:
caballeros, caballerizas,
tanques grandes como volcanes,
proyectiles ferruginosos.

Algo así le pasa también
al hipotético político
que conduce sin conducir
a multitudes invisibles.

Entonces cuando se me sube
la cabeza al humo, o más bien
el humo al pelo, el pelo al humo,
o me siento mayor que ayer,
la experiencia, con su tristeza,
me da un golpe de sopetón,
un torpe tirón de chaqueta,
y me derrumbo en mi verdad,
en mi verdad sin desmesura,
en mi pequeña y pasajera
verdad de ayer y todavía.

at a distance and from the side,
and in the front and in the back.

We are looking for a growing writer,
a critic the color of a fly
who every Sunday gilds
his little pill of fashion.
But nothing less happens
to the untimely military man
who commands and commands numbers,
regiments of paper:
gentlemen, grooms,
tanks big as volcanoes,
iron projectiles.

Something like that also happens
to the hypothetical politician
who leads without leading
the invisible multitudes.

Then when my head rises
to the smoke, or better yet
the smoke to the hair, the hair to the smoke,
or I feel older than yesterday,
experience, with its sadness,
delivers a sudden blow,
a clumsy tug on my jacket,
and I collapse into my truth,
into my truth, without excess,
into my small and fleeting
truth of yesterday and now.

Sale debajo del periódico
un criticante y se dispone
a dictar medidas de muerte
contra mi canto permanente.
No es sólo ese hombre de papel
sino que en su negra silueta
caben otros desesperados
que, con tenedor y tijera,
con oraciones y amuletos,
quieren que para complacerlos
se practiquen mis funerales.

No hablaré mal de estos cuantiosos:
recordaré de cuando en cuando
sus atributos animales
y no quiero tratarlos con,
ni tampoco tratarlos sin:
son merecedores del sol
como las uñas de mis pies,
pero no puedo estar de acuerdo
con la exquisita ceremonia
que destinaron pare mí
al declararme fallecido.

Por qué fallecer, me pregunto,
sin otra razón valedera
que satisfacer sus decretos,
sus operaciones sagradas,
dejar de ser sin más ni más
para que se mueran de gusto?

CERTAIN CONSPIRATORS

A critic comes out
from beneath the newspaper and begins,
a critic criticizing, who prepares
to dictate initiatives of death
for my abiding song.
It is not only that man of paper,
for in his black silhouette
desperate others squeeze in
who, with fork and scissors,
with speeches and amulets,
want to gratify themselves
by rehearsing my funerals.

I will not speak ill of these multitudes:
I will, from time to time, keep in mind
their animal attributes,
yet I do not want to deal with them,
nor deal without them:
they are deserving of sunlight
as are my toenails,
but I cannot go along
with the exquisite ceremony
they have set out for me
once they have declared me dead.

Why die, I ask myself,
for no good reason
other than to satisfy their decrees,
their sacred operations,
to cease being without further ado
just so they die of pleasure?

Cómo repite sus palabras!
Qué satisfecha es su estatura!
Hasta cuándo canta este diablo
un poco mejor que nosotros?
—dicen—mezclando con cuidado
la voz con los ojos al cielo
y la tinta con la estricnina.

Yo pienso darles esperanza,
dejarlos que acerquen las manos
al ataúd, hacerme el muerto,
y cuando las lágrimas salgan
de sus ojos de cocodrilo
resucitar cantando el canto,
el mismo canto que canté:
el que voy a seguir cantando
hasta que estos hijos de puta
resuelvan darse por vencidos
y acepten lo que se merecen:
un cementerio de papel.

How he repeats his words!
How smug his stature!
Until when will this devil sing
just a little better than we?
—they ask—mixing with caution
the voice with the eyes in the sky
and the ink with the strychnine.

I plan to offer them hope,
let them bring their hands
close to the coffin, pretend to be dead,
and when the tears pour out
of their crocodile eyes
to resuscitate singing the song,
the same song that I sang:
the one I will keep on singing
until those sons of a whore
decide to surrender in defeat
and accept what they deserve:
a cemetery of paper.

X

ESCRITORES

Canta Cortázar su novena
de imponente sombra argentina
en su iglesia de desterrado
y es difícil para los muchos
el espejo de este lenguaje
que se pasea por los días
cargado de besos veloces
escurriéndose como peces
para brillar sin fin sin par
en Cortázar, el pescador,
que pesca los escalofríos.

Del Perú cuyo rostro guarda
como cicatrices salobres
los versos de César Vallejo
surgió en mi edad un escritor
que floreció contando cuentos
del territorio tempestuoso,
y así escuché la nueva voz
de Vargas Llosa que contó
llorando sus cuentos de amor
y, sonriendo, los dolores
de su patria deshabitada.

(Yo soy el cronista irritado
que no escucha la serenata
porque tiene que hacer las cuentas
del siglo verde y su verdura,

X

Cortázar sings his novena
of imposing Argentine shadow
in his church of exile,
and it is difficult for many,
the mirror of this language
that walks through days
burdened with quick kisses
dripping like fish,
shining endlessly, without equal,
on Cortázar, the fisherman,
who fishes for the chills.

From Peru whose face guards
like brackish scars
the verses of César Vallejo
sprang in my age a writer
who blossomed telling stories
of stormy territory,
and so I listened to the new voice
of Vargas Llosa, who told
his tales of love, weeping,
and, smiling, the sorrows
of his decimated motherland.

(I am the irritable feature writer
who does not listen to the serenade
because he must compose the stories
of the green century and its lushness,

del siglo nocturno y su sombra,
del siglo de color de sangre.)

(Todo lo tengo que traer
al redondel de mis miradas
y ver donde salta el conejo
y donde rugen los leones.)

ALGUNOS

En Cuba rugía Fidel
con indiscutible grandeza,
pero sexuales escritores
se adueñaron de la cuestión:
sólo publicaron los besos
de una conducta irregular.

Ay qué chiquillos tan traviesos!

Pero no sintieron crecer
sino secretos paradisos:
dijeron: Esta boca es mía!
Como tenían sólo un ojo
estos algunos olvidaron
la magia terrestre de Cuba
y la insigne Revolución.

Estaban, sin duda, ocupados.

Mientras el azúcar crecía
y el humo de Cuba aromaba

of the nocturnal century and its shadow,
of the century the color of blood.)

(I must bring everything
into the circle of my eyes
and see where the rabbit leaps
and where the lions roar.)

SOME

In Cuba, Fidel roared
with indisputable grandeur,
but carnal writers
appropriated the matter:
they published only kisses
of their own bad behavior.

Oh, what mischievous boys!

They only perceived the growth
of secret paradises:
they said: This mouth is mine!
As they had only one eye
those someones forgot
the earthly magic of Cuba
and the renowned Revolution.

They were, no doubt, busy.

While the sugar grew
and the smoke of Cuba

con su tabaco el mundo entero,
crecían industrias extensas
o plantaciones de milagro,
ellos no vieron sino pies,
ombligos, falos pegajosos,
y cuando un ciclón derrotó
por un minuto a las Antillas
ciertos escritores unidos
determinaron exaltar
las pulgas más retroactivas
en el pubis surrealista.

Oh tú, Juan Rulfo de Anahuac,
o Carlos Fuentes de Morelia
o Miguel Otero Orinoco
o Revueltas de pecho en pelo
o Siqueiros cantando aún
con todo el mar de los colores
y la violencia celestial,
en qué quedamos, por favor?

Sábato, claro y subterráneo,
Onetti, cubierto de luna,
Roa Bastos, del Paraguay,
me pareció que ustedes eran
los transgresores del planeta,
los descubridores del mar,
pero el deber que compartimos
es llenar las panaderías
destinadas a la pobreza.
Ahora resulta que es mejor
el pornosófico monólogo!

scented with its tobacco the whole world,
industry spread far and wide
or miraculous plantations
arriving with only their feet,
navels, sticky phalluses,
and when for a single minute
a cyclone beat the Antilles
certain writers, in unison,
set themselves to exalting
the most reactionary fleas
in the surrealist pubis.

O you, Juan Rulfo de Anáhuac,
or Carlos Fuentes de Morelia
or Miguel Otero Orinoco
or Revueltas from chest to hair
or Siqueiros still singing
with the entire sea of colors
and celestial violence,
please, what is it to be?

Sábato, clear and subterranean,
Onetti, covered with moonlight,
Roa Bastos, of Paraguay,
it seemed to me that you were
the transgressors of the planet,
the discoverers of the sea,
but the duty that we share
is to fill the bakeries
meant for the poor.
Now, what is best,
the pornosophical monologue!

También en este tiempo tuvo
tiempo de nacer un volcán
que echaba fuego a borbotones
o, más bien dicho, este volcán
echaba sueños a caer
por las laderas de Colombia
y fueron las mil y una noches
saliendo de su boca mágica,
la erupción magna de mi tiempo:
en sus invenciones de arcilla,
sucios de barro y de lava,
nacieron para no morir
muchos hombres de carne y hueso.

ESCRITORES

Fueron así por estos años
levantando mis compañeros
un relato crespo y nocturno,
dilatado como el planeta,
lleno de acontecimientos,
de pueblos, calles, geografía,
y un idioma de tierra pura
con soledades y raíces.

A éstos yo canto y yo nombro,
no puedo contarlos a todos.

García Márquez

Also, at this time, it had
time to be born, a volcano
that was furiously throwing fire
or, that is to say, this volcano
was tossing dreams that fall
over the mountainsides of Colombia
and the thousand and some nights were
coming out of its magic mouth,
the grand eruption of my time:
in his inventions of clay,
dirty with mud and lava,
so many men of flesh and bone
were born to never die.

Writers

They were that way in those years,
my companions raising
a curly nighttime tale
vast as the planet,
full of what happens,
of peoples, streets, geography,
and a language of pure earth
with solitudes and roots.

These ones I sing and I name,
I cannot consider everyone.

Nosotros sudamericanos,
nosotros subamericanos,
por nuestra culpa y maleficio
vimos nuestros nombres por fin,
las sílabas de nuestra nieve
o el humo de nuestras cocinas
estudiados por otros hombres
en trenes que bajan de Hamburgo
o que suben desde Tarento.

Vienen de lejos

Oh cuánto se desenterró
debajo de nuestras campanas,
cuánto se supo de nosotros
porque hablaron mis compañeros
en sus libros de letra oscura
como si fueran caminando
por nuestro planeta harapiento.

Y los de la triste voz,
predecesores de la lluvia
con tormentos encadenados
desde el Paraguay lastimero
donde llora el urutaú.

Ay ausentes, ay sumergidas
tribus azules del Mayab,
indios de Chile derrotados
por una espada sifilítica.

We South Americans,
we lesser Americans,
in our blame and curse
saw our names ever after,
the syllables of our snow
or the smoke of our kitchens
studied by other men
on trains that descend from Hamburg
or climb from Taranto.

THEY COME FROM AFAR

Oh so much was unearthed
from beneath our bells,
so much was learned about us,
because my companions spoke
in their books of dark letters
as if they were walking
across our ragged planet.

And those of the sad voice,
precursors of the rain
with chained torments
from plaintive Paraguay
where the barn owl cries.

Oh, the absent, oh, the sunken
blue tribes of the Mayab,
indians of Chile defeated
by a syphilitic sword.

Ay reyes muertos, extendidos
en los surcos y en las terrazas,
acumulados por la muerte
hasta callar en el olvido,
esperando el germen del fuego,
de la guerrilla verdadera,
tal vez otra vez estáis vivos
en la escritura que publica
mi compañero manantial.

Por eso y por lo que canté
y me mantuve resurrecto
celebro al cronista de ahora
y lo declaro venerable:
ahora suenan las campanas
sobre tantísimo silencio
que se nos estaba pudriendo.
Y vinieron los escritores
a vengarse de los culpables,
es decir, del tiempo callado
y de sus cómplices amargos.

Cantando se funda la patria
y si no se sigue cantando
se muere la tierra en tus brazos
y esto lo vengo a proclamar
porque el amor es mi venganza.

Oh, dead kings, scattered
among the furrows and on terraces,
gathered in death,
to fall silent in oblivion,
waiting for the germ of the fire,
of the genuine guerrilla,
maybe you live again
in the script that reveals
my companion at the source.

For that reason and for what I sang
and, resurrected, kept on living,
I celebrate the chronicler of now
and I declare him venerable:
now, the bells sound
over all the silence
that was spoiling us.
And the writers came
to take revenge on the guilty,
that is to say, on silent time
and its bitter accomplices.

Singing, the motherland is found,
and if it does not go on singing
the earth dies in your arms,
and this I come to proclaim
because love is my revenge.

XI

Contra-azul

Cómo quitamos el azul,
la palabra azul, y qué haremos
sin tener nunca más azul?

A veces pienso que ocupó
demasiado sitio en mi casa,
en mi cielo, en mi poesía:
ya tengo bolsillos azules
y he llamado tantos azules
a poblar el pobre infinito
que poco a poco y sin saber
yo me fui poniendo azul
como si me hubieran pintado
el corazón y la camisa.

Atrás, animales azules,
fuera de mí, noche celeste,
quiero un aire color de tierra,
bestias de cuernos iracundos
que rompan el cielo y que caiga
sangre del cielo a borbotones:
quiero una Venus amarilla
saliendo de la espuma negra
y que los lagos se derramen
y se derroche su dulzura
hasta ver el fondo reseco
como un cráter de cicatrices.

XI

How do we free ourselves of blue,
the blue word, and what will we do
having no more blue?

At times I think it occupied
too much room in my house,
in my sky, in my poetry:
I already have blue pockets
and I have called so many blues
to populate the poor infinite
that little by little and without knowing it
I myself became blue
as if they had painted
my heart and my shirt.

Earlier, blue animals,
beyond me, light blue night,
I want air the color of earth,
beasts of irascible horns
that pierce the sky, so that the blood
of the sky falls in bubbles:
I want a yellow Venus
rising out of the black foam
and the lakes to spill outward
and their sweetness be squandered
until the dry bottom is seen
as a crater of scars.

FÍSICA

El amor como la resina
de un árbol colmado de sangre
cuelga su extraño olor a germen
del embeleso natural:
entra el mar en el extremismo
o la noche devoradora
se desploma sobre tu patria:
se desploma el alma en ti mismo,
suenan dos campanas de hueso
y no sucede sino el peso
de tu cuerpo otra vez vacío.

PROVERBIOS

El estímulo de la sombra
hizo brillar rastros oscuros,
huesos que el aire derribó
detrás de los ferrocarriles,
o simplemente estrellas negras
que nadie quiere ni conoce.
Ésa fue mi estación primera.

Tuve que hacer y adivinar
para vivir y subsistir,
tuve que trenzar el dolor
hasta sacar fuerza de donde
nadie podía sacar nada,
especialicé mi tristeza

PHYSICS

Love, like the resin
of a tree filled with blood,
hangs out its strange odor of the origin
of natural enchantment:
the sea goes to extremes
or the devoured night
breaks over your motherland:
your soul breaks inside you,
two bells of bone sound,
and nothing happens but the weight
of your body, empty once again.

PROVERBS

The stimulus of the shadow
made dark trails shine,
bones the air demolished
beyond the railways,
or simply black stars
that no one wants or knows.
That was my first season.

I had to make and prophesy
to live and survive,
I had to braid the pain
until finding strength where
no one was able to find anything,
I specialized my sadness,

y trabajando a la intemperie
endurecí mi viejo traje.
Ésa fue la estación segunda.

La tercera es ésta que vivo
contando y recontando mi alma,
seguro de tantos errores,
satisfecho de mis desvíos.

Si sirve o no mi corazón
que otros saquen la consecuencia.

El Viajero

Sobrecogido va el viajero
con tantas deudas a la vida,
sostenido por su escasez,
ido y venido por las ruedas
que constituyen su tesoro,
su pánico y su movimiento.

Ya son las ocho del verano.
Cruza un satélite la luz
con la tristeza plateada
de una abeja de precisión.

No tiene mi protagonista
ningún interés en el cielo:
va a dejar su mercadería
al mercado de Talcachifa
y mientras suma sus miserias

and working in the open
I toughened my old suit.
That was the second season.

The third is this that I live
telling and retelling my soul,
sure of so many mistakes,
at peace with my deviations.

Whether or not my heart helps
let others take on the consequences.

THE TRAVELER

Taken by surprise, the traveler travels
with so many debts in life,
sustained by what he lacks,
going and coming by the wheels
that are the whole of his treasure,
his panic, and his movement.

Already it is eight o'clock in summer.
A satellite traverses the light
with the silvery sadness
of a bee of accuracy.

My protagonist has
no interest in the sky:
he goes to leave his merchandise
at the market of Talcachifa,
and while he multiplies his miseries

en un coche destartalado
va entrando la noche en sus ojos,
en sus bolsillos, en sus manos,
y de pronto se siente negro:
lo ha devorado gradualmente
la soledad de la comarca.

Así es cada hombre en el camino:
salió de su casa blindado
por su destino patriarcal
y entre los números urgentes
se cuelan sábanas, recuerdos,
un transitorio escepticismo,
y aquel viajero crepitante
sin darse cuenta va borrando
su identidad y sus negocios
hasta que termina su viaje.

Y el que llegó ya no es ninguno.

FUNDACIONES

Llegué tan temprano a este mundo
que escogí un país inconcluso
donde aún no se conocían
los noruegos ni los tomates:
las calles estaban vacías
como si ya se hubieran ido
los que aún no habían llegado,
y aprendí a leer en los libros
que nadie había escrito aún:

in a rickety car,
the night enters his eyes,
his pockets, his hands,
and he soon feels black:
he has slowly been consumed
by the solitude of the land.

It is so with every man on the road:
he left home armored
with the destiny of his fathers,
and among the urgent numbers
are filtered bedsheets, memories,
a passing skepticism,
and that crackling traveler
without seeing it goes erasing
his identity and his business
until his journey ends.

And he who has arrived is no longer anybody.

FOUNDATIONS

I came so early into this world
that I chose an unfinished country
where even Norwegians and tomatoes
were still unknown:
the streets were empty
as if those not yet arrived
had already left,
and I learned to read from books
that no one had yet written:

no habían fundado la tierra
donde yo me puse a nacer.

Cuando mi padre hizo su casa
comprendí que no comprendía
y había construido un árbol:
era su idea del confort.

Primero viví en la raíz
luego en el follaje aprendí
poco a poco a volar más alto
en busca de aves y manzanas.
No sé cómo no tengo jaula,
ni voy vestido de plumero
cuando pasé toda mi infancia
paseándome de rama en rama.

Luego fundamos la ciudad
con exceso de callejuelas,
pero sin ningún habitante:
invitábamos a los zorros,
a los caballos, a las flores,
a los recuerdos ancestrales.

En vano en vano todo aquello:

no encontramos a nadie nunca
con quien jugar en una esquina.

Así fue de feliz mi infancia
que no se arregla todavía.

they had not founded the earth
where I set out to be born.

When my father built his house
I knew that he did not know
he had constructed a tree:
it was his idea of comfort.

I first lived in the root,
then among leaves I learned
little by little to fly higher
in search of birds and apples.
I don't know why I don't live in a cage,
or why I go about dressed in a feather duster
when I spent my whole childhood
hopping from branch to branch.

Then we founded the city
with too many alleys
but without a single habitant:
we invited the foxes,
the horses, the flowers,
the ancestral memories.

In vain in vain all of it:

we never ever found anyone
with whom to play on a corner.

My childhood was that happy
and still has not been set right.

Yo estuve tan mal conformado
que nunca pude aprender nada
y si no ladré es porque entonces
no me enseñaron a ladrar.
Y así me pasé la vida
entre bellezas naturales,
entre las islas y el olor
de las jovencitas salvajes:
a pesar de todo lo que hice
soy un esclavo de la tierra.

Por eso paso sin mirar
al lado de la maquinaria:
no sé el idioma del motor,
me asustan las televisiones,
los aeropuertos, las centrales
de dentaduras hidroeléctricas
y apenas si amo, en el invierno,
los antiguos trenes cansados
que van desde el Sur hacia el Norte
mezclando el humo con la lluvia.

Detengo aquí la flor y nata
de mi plural lapicería:
dejo el papel sobre la arena
y me voy detrás de un relámpago
que se metió bajo una piedra
disfrazado de coleóptero
y si no molesto a ninguno
me quedaré a vivir aquí
al lado de una lagartija.

I was so poorly formed,
never able to learn a thing,
and if I didn't bark it is because back then
they did not teach me to bark.
And so I spent my life
among natural beauties,
among islands and the odor
of wild adolescents:
in spite of everything I made,
I am a slave of the earth.

For that reason I pass right on by
without looking at machinery:
I don't know the engine's language,
televisions frighten me,
airports, power plants
with hydraulic teeth,
and I scarcely love, in winter,
the weary antique trains
that go from the South to the North
mixing their smoke with the rain.

Here I detain the flower and cream
of my plural shop of pens:
I left the paper on the sand
and I leave behind a lightning bolt
that slipped beneath a stone
disguised as a coleopteran,
and if no one minds
I will go on living here
beside a small lizard.

Tristísimo siglo

El siglo de los desterrados,
el libro de los desterrados,
el siglo pardo, el libro negro,
esto es lo que debo dejar
escrito y abierto en el libro,
desenterrándolo del siglo
y desangrándolo en el libro.

Porque yo viví el matorral
de los perdidos en la selva:
en la selva de los castigos.
Yo conté las manos cortadas
y las montañas de cenizas
y los sollozos separados
y los anteojos sin ojos
y los cabellos sin cabeza.

Luego busqué por el mundo
a quienes perdieron la patria
llevando donde las llevé
sus banderitas derrotadas
o sus estrellas de Jacob
o sus pobres fotografías.

Yo también conocí el destierro.

Pero, nacido caminante
volví con las manos vacías
a este mar que me reconoce,
pero son otros los aún,
los todavía cercenados,

The century of the exiled,
the book of the exiled,
the brown century, the black book,
this is what I must leave
written and open in the book,
exhuming it from the century
and bleeding it in the book.

Because I lived in the thicket
of the lost ones in the forest:
in the forest of the punishments
I recounted the severed hands
and the mountains of ash
and the separate sobs
and the eyeglasses without eyes
and the heads of hair missing a head.

Then I searched throughout the world
for whoever lost the motherland,
carrying where I carried
their small defeated flags
or their stars of Jacob
or their poor photographs.

I, too, knew exile.

But, a born traveler,
I returned with empty hands
to this sea that recognizes me,
but others are the "and yets,"
those still cut off,

los que siguen dejando atrás
sus amores y sus errores
pensando que tal vez tal vez
y sabiendo que nunca nunca
y así me tocó sollozar
este sollozo polvoriento
de los que perdieron la tierra
y celebrar con mis hermanos
(los que se quedaron allí)
las construcciones victoriosas,
las cosechas de panes nuevos.

EXILIOS

Unos por haber rechazado
lo que no amaban de su amor,
porque no aceptaron cambiar
de tiempo, cambiaron de tierra:

sus razones eran sus lágrimas.

Y otros cambiaron y vencieron
adelantando con la historia.

Y también tenían razón.

La verdad es que no hay verdad.

Pero yo en mi canto cantando
voy, y me cuentan los caminos
a cuántos han visto pasar

those who keep leaving behind
their loves and their mistakes,
thinking that maybe maybe
and knowing never never
and it was my turn to sob
this dusty wail
for those who lost the earth
and to celebrate with my brothers
(those who remained there)
the victorious buildings,
the harvests of new breads.

EXILES

Some, for having rejected
what they did not love about what they love,
because they did not agree to change
the time, changed the earth:

their reasons were their tears.

And others changed and won,
advancing with history.

And they, too, were right.

The truth is there is no truth.

But I move forward singing
my song, and the roads tell me
of the many they have seen pass

en este siglo de apátridas.
Y el poeta sigue cantando
tantas victorias y dolores
como si este pan turbulento
que comemos los de esta edad
tal vez fue amasado con tierra
bajo los pies ensangrentados,
tal vez fue amasado con sangre
el triste pan de la victoria.

LIBRO

Mi cuaderno de un año a un año
se ha llenado de viento y hojas,
caligrafía, cal, cebollas,
raíces y mujeres muertas.

Por qué tantas cosas pasaron
y por qué no pasaron otras?

Extraño incidente de amor,
del corazón embelesado
que no vino a inscribir su beso,
o bien el tren que se movió
a un planeta deshabitado
con tres fumadores adentro
capaces de ir y de volver
sin ventaja para ninguno,
sin desventaja para nadie.

in this century of people without a country.
And the poet keeps on singing
so many victories, so much pain,
as if this turbulent bread
we of the era consume
may have been kneaded with earth
under bloodied feet,
may have been kneaded with blood,
the sad bread of victory.

BOOK

From year to year my journal
has filled with wind and leaves,
calligraphy, lime, onions,
roots, and dead women.

Why have so many things happened
and why have others not happened?

Strange episode of love,
of the captivated heart
that never got to inscribe its kiss,
or else the train that traveled
with three smokers inside
to an uninhabited planet,
able to leave and to return
without benefiting anyone,
without harming anyone.

Y así se prueba que después
aprenderemos a volver
en forma desinteresada,
sin hacer nada aquí ni allí,
puesto que resulta muy caro
en los finales de este siglo
residir en cualquier planeta,
de tal manera que, ni modo:
no hay sitio aquí para los pobres,
ni menos aún en el cielo.

Así las bodas espaciales
de nuestros insectos terrestres
rompieron la razón al tiempo
que rompían la sinrazón:
como una cáscara de huevo
se quebró la tapa del mundo
y otra vez fuimos provincianos:
entre nosotros se sabía
cómo hacer calles en la tierra
y cómo amar y perseguir
y crucificar a tu hermano.
Ahora el interrogatorio
de la luz con la oscuridad
toma una nueva proporción:
la del miedo con esperanza
y la de la sabiduría
que tiene que cambiar de tiesto.

Yo me perdono de saber
lo poco que supe en mi vida,
pero no me lo perdonaron
los avestruces de mi edad.

Thus it is proved, only afterward
do we learn to come back
in a disinterested form,
doing nothing here or there,
for it turns out to be so costly
in the final trials of this century
to live on any planet,
so much so that, what can be done:
there is no place here for the poor,
and even less in the sky.

So the weddings in space
of our earthly insects
broke with justice as
they were breaking with the lack of justice:
the hard cover of the world cracked
like an eggshell
and again we inhabited the provinces:
together we knew
how to build streets on the earth
and how to love and to pursue
and to crucify your brother.
Now the interrogation
of the light by the darkness
takes on a new proportion:
the light of fear, with hope,
and of wisdom
that must change flowerpots.

I forgive myself for knowing
how little I knew in my life,
but the ostriches of my age
never forgave me for it.

Ellos siempre sabían más
porque metían la cabeza
en los diarios de los domingos.

Pero mi error más decidido
fue que entrara el agua en el rostro
de mis intensas letanías:
por las ventanas se divisa
mi corazón lleno de lluvia.

Porque nacer es una cosa
y otra cosa es el fin del mundo
con sus volcanes encendidos
que se propusieron parirte:
así pasó con mis destinos
desde las uvas de Parral
(donde nací sin ir más lejos)
hasta las montañas mojadas
con indios cargados de humo
y fuego verde en la cintura.

VIVIR CIEN AÑOS

Estos cien años los viví
transmigrando de guerra en guerra,
bebiendo la sangre en los libros,
en los periódicos, en la
televisión, en la casa,
en el tren, en la primavera,
en España de mis dolores.

They always knew more
because they buried their heads
in the Sunday papers.

But my most resolute mistake
was the water running down the face
of my passionate litanies:
through the windows it saw itself,
my heart full of rain.

Because being born is one thing,
and a whole other thing is the end of the world
with its fiery volcanoes
that proposed giving birth to you:
so it was with my destinies
from the grapes of Parral
(where I was born, going no farther)
to the damp mountains
with indians heavy with smoke
and green fire around the waist.

To Live One Hundred Years

Those one hundred years I lived
one body to the next, from war to war,
drinking the blood of the books,
of the newspapers, of the
television, of the house,
of the train, of the spring,
of the Spain of my sorrows.

Europa se olvidó de todo,
de la pintura y de los quesos,
de Rotterdam y de Rimbaud
para derramar sus racimos
y salpicarnos a nosotros,
americanos inocentes,
con la sangre de todo el mundo.

Oh Europa negra, codiciosa
como las serpientes hambrientas,
hasta se te ven las costillas
en tu moderna geografía
y entregas tu luz insensata
a otros soldados sempiternos
que se empeñan en enseñar
sin haber aprendido nunca:
sólo saben ensangrentar
la historia norteamericana.

Pero no se trata de tanto,
sino de mucho más aún,
no sólo de lo que vivimos
o de lo que viviremos
sino de cuál es la razón
de reventar lo que tuvimos,
de quebrar lo que sostenía
la copa de lo cristalino
y hundir el hocico en la sangre
insultándonos mutuamente.

Yo tantas preguntas me hice
que me fui a vivir a la orilla
del mar heroico y simultáneo

Europe forsook everything,
the painter and the cheeses,
Rotterdam and Rimbaud,
so as to pour its clusters
and spatter us,
innocent Americans,
with the blood of the whole world.

Oh, black Europe, greedy
like hungry serpents,
we see even your ribs
in your modern geography,
and you deliver your foolish light
to other perpetual warriors
who persist in teaching
without learning anything:
they only know how to steep in blood
the history of North America.

But it is not really about much
but much more yet,
not only about what we lived
or what we will live
but rather, what the reason is
for blowing up what we had,
for shattering what sustained
the glass of the crystalline lens
and sinking the snout in blood,
insulting us all, mutually.

I asked myself so many questions
that I went to live at the shore
of the heroic and simultaneous sea,

y tiré al agua las respuestas
para no pelearme con nadie,
hasta que ya no pregunté
y de todo un siglo de muerte
me pongo a escuchar lo que dice
el mar que no me dice nada.

EL MAR

Porque de tal manera el mar
me acostumbró a su poderío
que las palabras le faltaron:
no hizo nada más que existir.

(Fue su conducta arrolladora
la que condujo mi energía.)

Yo vi sostener el volumen
de su insistencia decidida
sin más interés que las olas
derrochadoras de blancura
y el convulso estanque instigado
por la sal y por las estrellas.

Es la verdad: no comprendí
ningún mensaje, sin embargo
su actividad se despeñaba,
sus torres de sal se rompían
golpeando la misma frontera
con tan amarga identidad
que me mantuve en las arenas

and I threw the answers into the water
to avoid fighting with anyone,
until I asked no more
and out of an entire century of death
I set myself the task of listening to what it says,
the sea, which says nothing to me.

THE SEA

For in that way the sea
accustomed me to its power,
which its words lacked:
it did nothing more than exist.

(Its rolling bearing was
what bore my energy.)

I witnessed the solidity
of its decisive insistence
with no more interest than waves
squandering their whiteness
and the convulsed pool caused
by the salt and the stars.

It is true: I understood
no message whatsoever, though
its action hurled itself down,
its towers of salt broke
striking the same frontier
with so much bitter identity
that I stayed in the sand,

despidiéndolo cada noche
y esperándolo cada día.

Sólo el océano existió.

Sólo su sangre y su tormento
fuera del bosque de mi vida.
Me expulsaron de las ciudades.

(Constato porque me lo exige
mi obligación más transparente
la resurrección de la envidia.)

Se fueron todas las mujeres
y en un punto muerto me hallaron,
indefenso, los envidiosos.

CANTO

Para los pueblos fue mi canto
escrito en la zona del mar
y viví entre el mar y los pueblos
como un centinela secreto
que defendía sus batallas
lleno de amor y de rumor:
porque soy el hombre sonoro,
testigo de las esperanzas
en este siglo asesinado,
cómplice de la humanidad
con mis hermanos asesinos.

taking my leave every night
and awaiting it every day.

Only the ocean existed.

Only its blood and its torment
outside the forest of my life.
They threw me out of the cities.

(I note this because it requires
my clearest duty,
the resurrection of envy.)

All the women left.
Then they found me, stopped cold,
defenseless, the envious ones.

SONG

For the people my song was
written in the region of the sea,
and I lived between the sea and the people
like a secret sentry
defending their battles,
full of love and rumor:
for it is I, the sonorous man,
witness to their hopes
in this assassinated century,
accomplice of humanity
with my murderous brothers.

Todos queríamos ganar.

Fue el siglo del participante,
de partidos y participios.

El mundo se nos terminaba
y continuábamos perdiendo
ganando más cada día.

Acompañamos a la tierra
en cada marea de amor
y la fuimos llenando de hombres
hasta que no cabían más
y llegaron los desde lejos
a apoderarse de cuanto hay.

Es triste historia esta tristeza.

Por eso la debo cantar.

Es temprano.
                    1970.
Estos treinta años de crepúsculo
que vienen, que se agregan solos
al largo día, estallarán
como cápsulas en el silencio,
flores o fuego, no lo sé.
Pero algo debe germinar,
crecer, latir entre nosotros:
hay que dejar establecida
la nueva ternura en el mundo.

We all wanted to win.

It was the century of the participant,
of parties and participles.

The world was finishing us
and we went on losing,
winning more each day.

We ran with the earth
in each tide of love,
and we filled her with people
until no more fit,
and from far away they arrived
to seize whatever there was.

It has a sad history, this sadness.

For that reason I must sing.

It is early.
       1970.
These thirty years of dusk
to come, only to be added
to the long day, will explode
like capsules in the silence,
flowers or fire, I do not know.
But something must sprout,
grow, beat among us:
we must leave deeply rooted
the new tenderness in the world.

Canto

Me morí con todos los muertos,
por eso pude revivir
empeñado en mi testimonio
y en mi esperanza irreductible.

Canto

Uno más, entre los mortales,
profetizo sin vacilar
que a pesar de este fin de mundo
sobrevive el hombre infinito.

Canto

Rompiendo los astros recientes,
golpeando metales furiosos
entre las estrellas futuras,
endurecidos de sufrir,
cansados de ir y de volver,
encontraremos la alegría
en el planeta más amargo.

SONG

I died with every death,
so I was able to live again
bound by my testimony
and by my unyielding hope.

SONG

One of many, among mortals,
I prophesy without wavering
that despite this world's end,
infinite man survives.

SONG

The newest heavenly bodies breaking,
furious metals beating
among future stars,
hardened by suffering,
tired of leaving and returning,
we will find happiness
on the most bitter planet.

Adiós

Tierra, te beso, y me despido.

GOODBYE

Earth, I kiss you, and say goodbye.

About the Author

Pablo Neruda was born Neftalí Ricardo Reyes Basoalto in Parral, Chile, in 1904. He served as consul in Burma and held diplomatic posts in various East Asian and European countries. In 1945, a few years after he joined the Communist Party, Neruda was elected to the Chilean Senate. Shortly thereafter, when Chile's political climate took a sudden turn to the right, Neruda fled to Mexico and lived as an exile for several years. He later established a permanent home at Isla Negra. In 1970 he was appointed Chile's ambassador to France, and in 1971 he was awarded the Nobel Prize in Literature. Pablo Neruda died in 1973.

About the Translator

William O'Daly has previously published seven books of the late and posthumous poetry of Pablo Neruda with Copper Canyon Press, as well as a chapbook of his own poems, *The Whale in the Web*. O'Daly was a finalist for the 2006 Quill Award in Poetry for *Still Another Day*, the first book of his Neruda series. A National Endowment for the Arts Fellow, he has worked as a literary and technical editor, a college professor, and an instructional designer, and his poems, translations, essays, and reviews have appeared in a wide range of magazines and anthologies. With co-author Han-ping Chin, he recently completed a historical novel, *This Earthly Life*, set during the Chinese Cultural Revolution. O'Daly lives with his wife and daughter in the Sierra Nevada foothills of California.

OTHER BOOKS BY PABLO NERUDA
FROM COPPER CANYON PRESS

Still Another Day
The Separate Rose
Winter Garden
Stones of the Sky
The Sea and the Bells
The Yellow Heart
The Book of Questions
The Hands of Day

The Chinese character for poetry is made up of two parts: "word" and "temple." It also serves as pressmark for Copper Canyon Press.

Since 1972, Copper Canyon Press has fostered the work of emerging, established, and world-renowned poets for an expanding audience. The Press thrives with the generous patronage of readers, writers, booksellers, librarians, teachers, students, and funders—everyone who shares the belief that poetry is vital to language and living.

Major funding has been provided by:
Anonymous (3)
Beroz Ferrell & The Point, LLC
Lannan Foundation
National Endowment for the Arts
Cynthia Lovelace Sears and Frank Buxton
Washington State Arts Commission

For information and catalogs:
COPPER CANYON PRESS
Post Office Box 271
Port Townsend, Washington 98368
360-385-4925
www.coppercanyonpress.org

This book was designed and typeset by Phil Kovacevich.
The typeface is Sabon, designed by Jan Tschichold in 1964.
Printed on archival-quality paper at McNaughton &
Gunn, Inc.